Homeruns and Jackpots
Baseball in Nevada

Written by
Tim Mueller

Olli –
Thanks so
much! For
the love of the
game!
Tim Mueller

Edited by Mark Souder

Cover Photo Credits

Front Cover: Reno Silver Sox Uniform by Charlie Johnston, all others taken by Tim Mueller
Back Cover: Frederick Green

ISBN: 978-0-615-27995-4

Library of Congress Control Number: 2009903650

First Printing: April 2009
Second Printing: January 2010

Published by Tim Mueller
PO Box 2831
Carson City, NV 89702

Printed in the USA
by Morris Publishing
3212 East Highway 30
Kearney, Nebraska 68847
1-800-650-7888

The Scorecard: Table of Contents

Acknowledgements

I would like to thank first of all my Lord and Savior Jesus Christ for helping me to have the fortitude, resilience and ability to write this book. Without His leading none of this would be possible.

I am indebted to so many people that have helped me along this journey of Homeruns and Jackpots: Baseball in Nevada. I would like to say thanks to my lovely wife Sue, without your support and love this book would not have been possible. Next up my editor, I would be amiss not give credit where credit is due, Mark Souder who spent countless hours working and reworking my broken sentence fragments, comma splices, inconsistencies and other errors. Thanks also to Mark's wife, Christina who allowed her husband to help me unselfishly whenever I needed it.

Thanks Don Logan for writing my foreword. I appreciate your willingness to help me without much prodding. Thanks for your time I know your schedule especially in March begins to get very busy. Thanks for your help!

Tony Gwynn for allowing me to interview you it was a surreal experience to me as you are my favorite player and to interview you was an amazing experience. Ray Fosse thanks for talking with me about your playing days in Reno. What a journey! Thanks to you both for allowing me to print your quotes on my back cover.

Matt Brown, Editor of Nevada Magazine thanks for writing a byline for my book. It helped me to stay focused and to finish the race. Charlie Johnston thanks for the great photo of Beasley's Uniform.

Jim Gemma for quenching my thirst of knowledge of the Las Vegas 51s thanks also for providing me input, photos and stats.TJ Lasita of the Reno Aces thanks for providing helpful answers to all of my questions.

Bob Stewart fellow author, former Scoutmaster and friend, thanks for your loyal consistent support during the long duration of this project.

The late Dr. Bud Beasley who was like a surrogate father to me he guided me and helped me to learn how to talk with people how to interact and taught me how to love the game the way he did. Also many thanks for the 1948 Silver Sox Uniform. Mr. Murray Olderman who allowed me the use of the cartoon he drew of Bud Beasley in 1947. It was a pleasure to talk with you.

The late Rollan Melton who took a risk on me and printed me in his column without his assistance my phone would not have begun to ring. Ty Cobb the writer who allowed me in and showed me some of what he knew.

Debbie Gallas of the Oakland A's for granting me the press credentials that I requested. Susan Webner of the Arizona Diamondbacks for providing photos and information. Gary Powers of the University of Nevada he allowed me into his coaching world on many, many occasions. The Society of American Baseball Research (SABR) helped me to learn about the nuances of the game and how to write about them.

Kathy War from the UNLV Special Collections Library thanks for finding the photos of Cashman Field. Patricia Kelly from the National Baseball Hall of Fame it was a pleasure working with you. Jeffrey Kintop from the Nevada State Library and Archives thanks for the O'Callaghan photo.

I know that I have unintentionally left some people out my apologies to you.

I was spurred to continue this book through all of your kindness, support and responses to my requests for information. This book is as much yours as it is mine. Thanks again!!

Batting Practice: Foreword

By Don Logan

When people think of the "Silver State" of Nevada, the first things that likely comes to mind are the bright lights of the "fabulous strip," the charm of "the Biggest Little City in the World" or the breathtaking splendor of Lake Tahoe. In the world of sports, people associate Nevada with Vegas betting, championship boxing, the Runnin' Rebels or the Wolf Pack. Baseball is probably one of the last things that come to mind.

Considering baseball in Nevada, one's mind can wander in many directions: playing little league on dusty fields looking forward to a post game snack, playing softball with your friends a couple nights a week, watching the local high school or legion teams play on sun baked breezy evenings, or as like I do taking in a Pacific Coast League game at beautiful Cashman Field.

My introduction to the greatest game on earth occurred in 1964 when I was five years old and we went to Moana Stadium to watch the Reno Silver Sox. My father was a teacher at that time and attended the University of Nevada for summer school to earn a masters degree. Being from Tonopah, where there was not a grass field, Moana was beautiful. Later that summer we went to San Francisco to watch the Giants and Dodgers at Candlestick Park. It was at Candlestick watching Willie Mays, Willie McCovey and the rest of the Giants that a lifelong love affair began with the game of baseball and the men in black and orange.

From that point on I spent countless nights lying in the front seat of our car in the driveway with the radio tuned to KMJ 580 AM from Fresno. They carried all the Giant games and had the exceptionally talented Russ Hodges and Lon Simmons calling the play-by-play. The signal was great at night but a little shaky during the day, but a little static was no big deal.

As I got older and began to play, my love for the game intensified. We had no high school baseball team but played fast pitch softball from April through July. All the while, I listened to as many Giant games as possible. If I missed a game, my dad's good friend Joe Friel would fill me in on the scores, as he was always listening. Since Joe was a huge Dodger fan I didn't develop the disdain for the Dodgers that most Giant fans did, but rather a competitive respect. Seeing how rude and crude some Giant fans are when it comes to the Dodgers, I'm thankful for that and really would like to see Giant fans class it up a bit.

After high school I attended Dixie Junior College and Utah State University, where I got to play my first organized baseball games. After graduating from Utah State, and with no major league showing any interest, I decided to attend law school with designs on becoming a player agent.

Attending law school in Sacramento was a great thing because I was only 90 minutes away from Candlestick where I attended many games. It was there I met Giants owner Bob Lurie who told me baseball didn't need more agents but more executives. I left law school and began looking for a job in pro baseball. That was the fall of 1983 and I was fortunate that Joe Hawk responded to my inquiry about a position with the Las Vegas Stars who had just completed their first season after relocating from Spokane. Joe set up an interview with General Manager Larry Koentopp and I was hired as an account executive.

Twenty five years later I am the President and GM of the Las Vegas 51s (we changed the name from Stars in 2001) and have become somewhat of a guardian of baseball in Las Vegas and the state of Nevada. Though I wanted to pursue a career as a player, I am probably best suited for my current role.

I've had the good fortune of watching and getting to know players like John Kruk, Bruce Bochy, Ozzie Guillen, Shane Mack, Benito Santiago, Sandy and Roberto Alomar, Carlos Baerga, Joey Cora, Andy Benes, Derrek Lee, Eric Gagne, Russell Martin, Matt Kemp and James Loney, just to name a few. These players and those associated at all levels of the game are what make baseball so special.

Nevada has made an impact on baseball at both the professional and amateur level. Players like Greg Maddux, Mike

Maddux, Mike Morgan, Matt Williams, Marty Barrett and Rod Scurry have been quality long term major league players. Fred Dallimore and Gary Powers have built nationally ranked programs at UNLV and at Nevada. Tim Chambers has won a national Junior College Championship at the College of Southern Nevada, Ron McNutt had a top notch championship program at Carson City High and Roger Fairless had multiple championship teams at both Valley and Green Valley High School

Take time and enjoy the detailed stories of these players and coaches and many others in this book. Tim Mueller poured his heart and soul into this effort and deserves a hearty thank you from everyone involved, both past and present, for his work in writing this book about baseball in Nevada.

Don Logan

President / General Manager
Las Vegas 51s

March 2009

Taking Infield: Introduction

Baseball is a game of romance, numbers and history. This is an unbeatable combination, one unmatched in sport. The smell of freshly cut grass, the popping of a baseball into a leather glove, the crack of the bat, the dull whisper of player chatter, coaches barking out calls, lawn sprinklers twirling, a lawnmower cutting, the buzz of the stadium lights, and the subtle rustle of spectators arriving create a unique atmosphere like none other on Earth.

My journey has taken me from being a casual fan to serious fan to a somewhat obsessive fan. When I started I was just a fan. You know the type—you get to the game and you find your seat and you just watch. You don't give it too much thought. You just sit, and that is all of the thinking you do. I became a baseball fan when I was about six. At the time my family lived in Southern California, and we (mostly) were Los Angeles Dodger fans. Some of the earliest memories I have of baseball are listening to Vin Scully call balls and strikes. It was a time when I believed the game was pure, and players played the game because they loved it...not for the money. Whether or not this was truly the case is not the important thing; what is important is that it started my lifelong love affair with baseball. I remember buying a few packages of baseball cards off the ice cream truck for only a dime. The joy of opening those cards was a feeling that I will remember my entire life, and it really drew me into the game.

The first Major League game I went to was played between the Cincinnati Reds and the Dodgers. The year was 1974. The "Big Red Machine" of the Reds was firing on all cylinders, and the Dodgers were just trying to compete. Steve Garvey, the first baseman of the Dodgers, was my favorite player, and I was hooked! We went to another game in 1975; this time between the St. Louis Cardinals and the Dodgers. I saw Lou Brock swipe a bag or two.

In 1975 my family moved to Reno, Nevada, which I thought was like moving to Siberia in terms of what baseball had to offer.

Soon I learned that Reno had a team that played in the class A California League, named the Reno Padres. I would ride my red

Schwinn Sting Ray bicycle through a hole in a fence and through a dusty field to Moana Lane and into the ballpark. I bought a season youth pass in 1984 for $10 from general manager Harry Platt, and I was ready for a summer of great baseball memories. The Reno Padres had an "unofficial" rule that if you shagged foul balls and brought them back, you received two tickets to an upcoming baseball game. I earned a lot of extra tickets for family and friends and had lots of fun hanging out at Moana Stadium.

Another extremely enjoyable part of the experience was getting autographs. After passing through the turnstile, I usually started with buying a scorecard for 25 cents. On it I would mark off the best players according to their stats. I always checked out the visiting roster first, as I knew they would only be in town for a few days. Not only that, but a player might get called up to play at the next level, and I might not have the chance to see him again. I would then station myself by the visiting locker room entrance and start asking visiting team members for their autographs. This method worked well, as I was able to secure the autographs of Roberto Alomar, Mike Piazza and about 200 others. As the game progressed and bats got broken, I would make a note on my scorecard and ask the appropriate player after the game for his bat. My most memorable bat experience was when I asked Marc Newfield for his broken bat. Since he was a top prospect at the time, I asked him to autograph it. He obliged, and I have kept the bat to this day.

I always had a wonderful time at Moana Stadium and continue to have fond memories of my time spent at the historic yard on Moana Lane.

My love of the game took a brief hiatus while I earned my Eagle Scout award and went through the rigors of public education. But when I began attending the University of Nevada, Reno, I began to follow the game in a new way. I started to earn a little more money and had more flexibility, and I was able to get to a game once in a while in San Francisco, at Candlestick Park. I attended my first collegiate baseball game in 1991 at Peccole Park, home of the University of Nevada's Wolf Pack baseball team. I also had a class with University of Nevada second baseman Dean Bonfigli, and we became friends.

Through Dean's friendship, I learned about what a team goes through from the first drills through the end of the season. I found out about all the ups and downs through the eyes of an insider. It provided me with a unique perspective, one that I had not been privy to, and got me to think about baseball from a more educated standpoint. I felt like I was part of the team without stepping out onto the field. This experience really created a hunger within me for the complexities of the game and led me to writing this book.

The first game of the "Tim Mueller Serious Fan Era" began on March 26, 1996, at the Stanford vs. Nevada game at Peccole Park. I was not all that concerned whether Nevada would win the game (but they did, and it was great!). I was more interested in how the game was being played, what the coaches and players were discussing, what the crowd was feeling and other nuances of the game...

These nuances of the game often prepare baseball players on how to live life. In life, it is necessary to do something by action to reach a goal. In baseball, you must be able to swing the bat with skill to get a base hit; once on base, you need to read the proper sign from your coach. After you have picked up the sign, if you have speed, you steel second base. You then await further instructions. In life, you either wait or give instructions, depending on your position.

Emotions play a tremendous role in baseball. It can be something as subtle as a called fourth ball, an errant pick-off throw to first, a yelling fan or coach or parent or a gust of wind that carries a ball over the outfield fence. Baseball, by many accounts, is a game of inches, execution, speed, timing, and of preparedness. Being well trained and coached is often what determines winners and losers. I am a believer that sometimes heart and attitude can win championships. Talent gets you there, but your heart makes you a winner.

I had the great privilege to attend several games a member of the press. This provided me a new perspective and the ability to learn the game anew. It was fun! I started to think some of the future and whether or not I could be granted a press credential to games in the Major Leagues. I tried and was granted credentials for two Oakland A's games—one against my favorite team, the San Diego Padres, and the other against the Arizona Diamondbacks. I must give credit where credit is due; this book would not be possible without the generosity of players, coaches and friends. In the years that followed, I would be granted a few other credentials. I found this to be the best way to learn and write about the sport that I loved from a vantage point that few others have been afforded the opportunity.

This book offers you information that has not been published before. Nevada has created a unique environment in which the game of baseball is linked to many communities, both on and off the field. Baseball has survived in some locations and died in others. The ultimate success or failure of a baseball team is often tied to the local economy. In gathering information for this book, I've interviewed players, fans, coaches and government officials. These include a range of folks, from the late guru of minor league baseball, Dr. Bud Beasley, to former New York Yankees pitcher Darrell Rasner, Jr. I've conducted extensive research and travel to ensure that the facts presented are as accurate as possible. I must add one disclaimer: this project has been large, and at times overwhelming. I apologize up front for any errors or omissions. They were not intentional. I have included an address in the back of the book where I urge you to send updated or corrected information. Please take the opportunity to write and comment; I would enjoy hearing from you. I hope you enjoy your journey through *Homeruns and Jackpots: Baseball in Nevada* as much as I did!

McGill, Nevada Scoreboard, Taken by the Author

1st Inning: The Uniform

As I wandered through this project I sometimes did not have a plan. I would just show up in a certain place and find something unexpected. One such place was Douglas County. I talked with the curator of the museum and discussed that I was writing a book about baseball in Nevada she said wait a couple of minutes, she had something she wanted to show me. She came back with a uniform that was from the 1920's I could not believe it. It was the first historical uniform that I had seen. I touched it and felt it and wrote about it...it seemed like it was more than just cloth...it was part of someone's life a person that I would not know, but a person that I did know through the game of baseball. This is part of the fabric of the sport that I love more than any other.

An author never knows where the research will take him. The one thing I learned about writing a book is that there are unplanned turns and twists. It was up to me to stay on course One day I was conducting some research in Douglas County, Nevada. I mentioned that I was writing a book about baseball in Nevada, and as a result, I was fortunate to see a 1920's uniform.

As I felt the uniform it made me feel honor, nostalgia, pride, dignity, character, purity and most importantly love. The Carson Valley uniform represented something bigger than baseball. It represented a dream...a dream of making it to "the Show"...a dream of having a successful and fulfilling life not just on the field but off. I have no doubt that this uniform prepared whoever wore it for the many aspects of life...to say that baseball is a training ground for life might be an over simplification but, I think it is worthy of consideration.

I felt the need to climb inside the uniform to feel the woolen cloth scratch my skin. I felt lured to the uniform to see if I could capture some of the history that it held. The uniform was an awesome treasure and I was the finder. Now it was time to explore its rich history and tradition. The material felt like it was an inch thick. It was coarse and rough to the touch, like sandpaper. I felt sorry for the person who wore it during the 1920's, especially during a hot Nevada summer day. The uniform was stained. It smelled of dust and of being old.

I wanted to put on the uniform even though I couldn't I imagined what 1920's possibly were; an era of fun and frolic. The only problem was this uniform just would not fit me. I didn't know why...

Carson Valley Uniform c. 1920

Unfortunately, the uniform would not fit because it was worn by the late Roy Edwin Smith of Carson Valley. In my opinion Mr. Roy Smith had played baseball "as good as the young Detroit Tigers Ty Cobb". Roy possibly even dreamed of playing one day in "the Show".

In the 1920's Nevada was wide open and inviting. It was easy to start a life and a family. It was easy to learn who you were and what you would want to do with your life. Time was easier to manage. You didn't need to worry about locking your house or your car (most people didn't even bother with a car). Life was simpler and less hurried. It would have been a unique and exciting time to live in.

On yet another journey this one to the town of Eureka, Nevada I came across a second uniform. This one was much different in texture than the first. It was more of a mix of cotton and wool and was much lighter. It was made at the A.G. Spalding factory in Chicago.

This uniform was worn by a member of the Rebaleati family around 1900. This uniform was in much better condition than the first. There was a gray "E" diamond on the shoulder. "EUREKA" was proudly spelled out down the front of the uniform. The uniform was full of pride and full of spirit. I was amazed by the rush of emotions that I felt. I wanted to put it on also, but knew that there would be no way that I could fit into the shoes of the one who wore it.

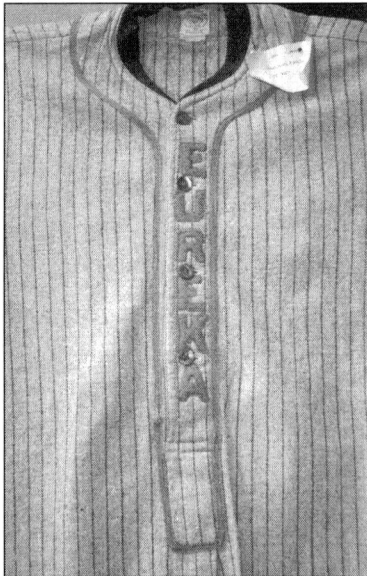

Eureka Uniform c. 1900

I could make an attempt to wear it, but I would not be able to do it justice. I am a "tech nerd" living in the 21st century and the man who wore it around 1900 was a "blue collar miner" who worked extremely long days in a rural far-flung Central Nevada mining community. I'm sure that the man worked at least 10 hour days and more often 12 hour days. He worked and worked and worked, and not by a computer or in an air conditioned office either. He was a man's man, a real worker. He probably played baseball the same way he lived, sweating every out as if it was his last. It would have been a pleasure to watch him play a game in the dusty 1900 town of Eureka, Nevada.

In sharp contrast, today's modern uniform is made of 100% polyester. Many teams also have multiple uniforms and now there are special limited edition uniforms for special events like the All-Star game and World Series. The song "Where have you gone Joe DiMaggio" brings back thoughts of where tradition and values have gone. When MTV and KISS became popular the values and politeness of society were deleted from its memory like losing a precious document or photo in a computer crash. I'm babbling now, but you know where I stand...

I'm a traditionalist. I say if ain't broke don't fix it. In the movie "Field of Dreams," the sand lot game is about as perfect as baseball gets and it was that way in 1918. Why did it have to change?

That is most likely the reason that I enjoy baseball so much. It ties the past into the present. You have time to soak it in. It is a great game.

2nd Inning: Bud Beasley

The late Dr. Bud Beasley was energetic, kind, candid and helpful. Dr. Beasley was born on December 8, 1910, in a sod house on a ranch near the town of Melrose, New Mexico. From those very humble beginnings, Beasley became "the guru of Minor League Baseball; he knew everybody," according to Robert "Buzz" Knudson. Beasley graduated from Santa Cruz High School, California, and from the University of Nevada in 1934. He then received his doctorate in education from Columbia University. He started working at Reno High School in 1936. Between teaching classes and coaching baseball, Beasley played with the Sacramento Solons and the Seattle Rainers of the Pacific Coast League. In addition, in the early 1930s, Beasley played on the Inter-Fraternity and Reno Garage baseball teams during the summers he schooled at Nevada.

Before deciding to attend the University of Nevada, Beasley had the chance to attend the University of California. "I had a scholarship to Cal for baseball, but my brother talked me out of it, because he didn't like Cal. I played under an assumed name, 'Blake,' as there was still a possibility that I might go to college. My football coach at Santa Cruz High was the great 'Rabbit' Bradshaw, and he kept talking to me about the University of Nevada. I had such a great respect for him that I enrolled at the University of Nevada in 1930."

Prior to coming to Nevada in 1930, Beasley played in the San Francisco city leagues. San Francisco often had very strong winter baseball leagues during this era. Beasley played against Joe DiMaggio in the original California State League (1928–1929). In the 1930s, Joe, Vince and Dom DiMaggio played in the Pacific Coast League. Beasley remembered Joe DiMaggio fondly. "I played against Joe. I had a respect for him. I hate to say this, but this was before Joe D became Joe D. He was just one of the ballplayers. None of us would have picked him to make the Majors." Joe DiMaggio developed into a great player under the watchful eye of Lefty O'Doul of the San Francisco Seals.

Lefty helped him learn how to run and hit and really turned him into the great ballplayer he became.

Beasley had a love of the game that was unmatched. He paid for the very first set of baseball uniforms for Reno High School out of his own pocket. During the summer months, Beasley would live in the San Francisco Bay Area and play as much baseball as he could. In the summer of 1934, he came back and played for the semi-pro Reno Garage team owned by Jack Threlkel. "Because I was playing for Jack, I got to use the field for the high school team. I was also able to get some equipment from Jack as well," Beasley reminisced. He continued coaching baseball at Reno High School during the same years that he played at the semi-pro level in the San Francisco Bay Area.

Beasley was very instrumental in the development of Nevada high school baseball. Over the years, he coached thousands of baseball players at Reno High School, including Dan Hellman, Carl Moroon, Fred Dallimore, Larry McKinnen and Fred Newshower. According to Beasley, "Fred Dallimore was one of my best pitchers. His dad caught for me also." Beasley also mentioned that it would be very easy to forget some great players; after all, he coached for 40 seasons!

The Reno High School teams played the Nevada State Prison and University of Nevada Fraternity ball clubs. It was often very difficult finding teams to play during the early 1950s, as there were very few teams in Northern Nevada. During this era, the Reno High School team played the Reno Silver Sox. Beasley recalled this era in this way: "The first priority was to get a crowd and to make money. Dan Hellman pitched that game. He was so good of a pitcher that I couldn't pitch him against high schools. He was great! Hellman struck out 18 or 20 batters." The Silver Sox eventually prevailed and beat Reno High in 10 innings.

Beasley was constantly looking for ways to help his Reno High School team. When the Stead Air Base closed in 1966, the military decided to get rid of their equipment by burying uniforms and other equipment in trenches. Some uniforms were still new and in boxes, yet the Air Base couldn't sell or give them away because the local sporting goods stores would not allow it. Air Base personnel knew Beasley coached a ball club, so he struck a deal with them.

Instead of burying the equipment, they simply dumped it off their truck, and Coach Beasley picked it up off the street. The Air Base staff didn't want Beasley to get caught with the uniforms and other equipment. Beasley got so many uniforms and other equipment in this fashion that he had plenty of equipment for the next 10 years.

Dr. Beasley is indeed the guru of Minor League Baseball in Nevada. He knew of or met so many baseball people, including Ty Cobb (the player), Ty Cobb (the writer), Babe Ruth, Chuck Conners, Joe DiMaggio, Lilo Marcucci, Bill Schuster, Casey Stengel, Lefty O'Doul, Jackie Robinson, Earl Sheely, Billy Martin, Jo Jo White, Wally Westlake, Joe Marti, Tony Fretias, Lefty Gomez, Dale Reynolds, Grover Cleveland Alexander, Satchel Paige, Walter Johnson and Sam Spade.

Great Experiences from the Pacific Coast League

While playing in the Pacific Coast League (PCL), Beasley met many great baseball players. "I first met Ty Cobb [the player] when I was playing on the Sacramento Solons. He opened the season by throwing out the first pitch. He took off his coat and hat, borrowed my baseball cap and threw out the first ball. Ty Cobb said 'You're from Reno; I live at Lake Tahoe.'" Beasley continued, "I had him come down a few times to visit the children's home in Carson City. He would sign baseballs and talk with the kids." Beasley also met Babe Ruth when he was playing for the Seattle Rainers of the Pacific Coast League; this was shortly before Ruth died. It greatly saddened Beasley to see Babe Ruth at that time, because Beasley had remembered him as a very strong man. Ruth didn't even weigh 100 pounds, he could barely be understood, and it was obvious that he wasn't going to live much longer. "That did something to me seeing that," Beasley said.

Beasley also met Chuck Conners, who played "The Rifleman" on television. Conners played on the Hollywood Stars when Beasley was with the Solons. Every now and then Conners would recite the famous baseball poem "Casey at the Bat," originally written by Ernest L. Thayer. After seeing how popular it was with the fans, Beasley made it part of his daily routine as well. Reciting the poem just added to the already legendary personality of Bud Beasley.

Bud Beasley Cartoon, July 9, 1947
Courtesy: Murray Olderman

Beasley was also affectionately known as the "Clown of the Pacific Coast League." Beasley was usually a showman, both on and off the field. He may have been one of the best pranksters of his day. Beasley was also a very good pitcher as well; in 1947, he led the league in strikeouts and wins. In 1945, he pitched the longest game in professional baseball, a 17-inning contest. He even went on to score the winning run and made it into *The Sporting News*. Beasley made the

Coast League All-Star Game in 1947, which was played at Los Angeles's Wrigley Field. Beasley remembered, "I drew a lot of fans." In 1949, he pitched the last game played at Sacramento's Solon Field.

Bill Schuster, who played with the Chicago Cubs and L.A. Dodgers, made a tremendous impact on the young and often impressionable Beasley. "Everything funny and comical that I did I modeled after him [Schuster]. When we played against each other, neither one of us would allow the other to out-showboat the other. Once while playing in Los Angeles at Wrigley Field, the league leader in stolen bases was on first. I was pitching. This guy was going to steal on me, and I thought there is no way this guy is going to steal on me. First, I gave him the decoy move. I led him to believe that was my good move, and then I gave him the really good move; I kept him close by throwing over there five times. Bill was at the plate, and I didn't throw him a pitch; he then went to first with the bat. He did this to out-showboat me. The crowd had a big laugh, and it showed up in the papers. During the 1950s, he was my manager in the Canadian League."

While playing in the PCL, Beasley met one of the best managers in Major League history, Casey Stengel. Beasley related one story involving the famous manager, and he told it in a way that made it seem like this could have taken place just last week. "Casey and his wife were having breakfast in the hotel dining room. When they brought me my check, I said, 'Take it over there and my dad [Stengel] will take care of it.' The waitress took it over. Casey looks at it; the waitress says, 'That guy over there pointing at me sent it over,' and he took care of it."

Beasley continued, "On 'Casey Stengel Night' at an Oakland Acorns game, they gave Casey a Cadillac, and he said, 'How am I going to get it home? My wife already has one.' After Casey was managing with the Yankees, I did some post-graduate work at Columbia University. I knew New York State backwards and forwards. I asked Casey, 'How about taking me back as your chauffeur?' Casey said, 'I'll be dammed if I'll let a left-hander drive my car.' He was a real character! Casey mocked all of my crazy windups." Beasley laughed often when he related this story. "Casey was like a dad to me," he said.

Dick Bartell was Beasley's manager on the Sacramento Solons squad. Bartell had a poor reputation with his players and had a difficult time understanding why Beasley clowned around. Bartell also had a strong love of baseball and always had the strong desire to bat. At one batting practice, the Solons only had 40 minutes to bat, and Bartell used up 20 of them. Beasley recalled this humorous tale, "I'm throwing batting practice. My teammates gave me a grapefruit that was painted white to throw at him. I threw it and when he hit it, the grapefruit spattered and got all over him." Bartell then wanted to sell "Beas" right away; however, team management wanted to keep him because he was such a tremendous drawing card. On another occasion, Bartell said not to throw a ball above anybody or that player would be fined $100. Beasley got the call to come into a ballgame, and Bartell told him to keep the ball down. Beasley, still being the practical joker, rolled the next pitch on the ground all the way to home plate. That day Beasley was sold outright to Seattle.

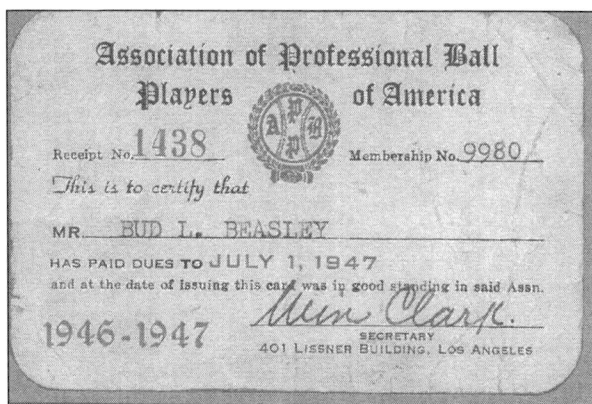

Bud Beasley's Association of Professional Ball Players ID
(Bud Beasley Collection)

Reno Garage and a Man Named Threlkel

Beasley played on Jack Threlkel's Reno Garage teams in the 1930s and 1940s. Threlkel was very big during this time. He owned a fabulous park, called Threlkel Park, in Reno (near the intersection of Interstate 80 and US 395), where the playing surface was as good as any ballpark in the state. He had a strong semi-pro team. The players got paid directly out of the gate proceeds at the end of the season. Threlkel loved baseball and loved that park with all his heart. He maintained the field himself. He put a lot of money into the stadium, uniforms and travel. He even hired his own umpires. They played Saturday night and Sunday afternoon games and paid visiting teams great guarantees to come play.

Threkel Park c. 1940 (Source: Bud Beasley Collection)

Bud Beasley recalled that Jack Threlkel was also a very competitive man. He would never sit in the dugout; instead he would sit in foul territory and give signals to the players from there. "He was temperamental and would often yell at the umpires and then buy them a steak dinner," Beasley recalled. Threlkel brought in the best baseball players that money could buy. He had the best parking garage in town across the street from the Majestic Theater.

Northern Nevada baseball owes a lot to Jack Threlkel. Single-handily he kept the game alive and brought in the best teams, such as the House of David. He shared the ballpark with the Reno High and American Legion teams. Threlkel had played second base as a youngster and was quite good. Beasley remembered, "He could hit infield practice with no problem, so he had obviously played before. He always wore a suit and hat to the games. He hit fielding practice when I first played. If there was a good player available anywhere, he would try to sign him. He spared no expense. You have to give him credit. He bought the best uniforms and was the first to have lights at his park."

Satchel Paige and his House of David team played against the Reno Garage around 1937. Since the House of David was short on pitching, Beasley traveled with the team for a few weeks. Each year, the House of David stopped in Reno. They were a big drawing card, and the team always would play at Threlkel Park. "I could remember battling against the great Satchel Paige. He would throw up those big size 14 shoes. He had a great kick and was tough. He was a very likable, very congenial fellow," Beasley reminisced.

Beasley shared the following memories about playing baseball in Reno, "Although Moana was the first ballpark in Reno, Threlkel's park was much better. He had a chicken and turkey pen in right field. About 350 feet down the line. Every once in a while you would hear some noise come out of the pen. Threlkel was a rancher first and businessman second. He had the pen for the eggs. He ran the garage and hired all of the ballplayers to work in the garage."

Beasley Is Back!

Beasley played with the Reno Garage until 1944. Then he joined the PCL. He came back to Reno in the late 1950s to manage the Reno Garage team. In 1947, Beasley served in an advisory role to the Reno Silver Sox. Beasley was involved with baseball on many different fronts in Northern Nevada. His energy and love of the game was always in the forefront.

Beasley played in the Canadian League until 1955. He continued playing with the Stockton Old Timers for about five more years. All of Stockton's players were ex-pro baseball players who were 35 years old or older. San Francisco, Lodi, San Jose and Stockton all had teams. Beasley played just for fun from the late 1950s to early 1960s.

Beasley simply loved to have fun. "I've got to have fun. I was doing it primarily for my own enjoyment, and I learned that the crowds enjoyed it. The crowd loved the screwy things that I did. Once I filled my glove with talcum powder. I pitched out of a smokescreen by pounding the glove. I got away with it for two or three innings." Beasley was always on the lookout for new props to insert into his show. On a road trip to Edmonton, Canada, Beasley picked up a chunk of coal walking in from the bullpen. He put the coal in his jacket pocket. The ump threw Beasley a new ball as the previous hitter had hit a home run. Beasley took his warm-up tosses with the new ball. Then "I threw the lump of coal to the catcher. Nobody knew it was coming. The pitch was called a strike, the ump took away the coal and let the strike stand. The crowd laughed. I got away with it because I was able to draw a crowd. As long as I wasn't hurting the other team, I could get away with it."

Beasley respected the hitters the most, and he was often asked if he was superstitious. He would say, "Yeah I'm superstitious of anyone who comes up with a bat in his hand."

Beasley coached baseball at Reno High School from 1936 to 1976, longer than any coach in Nevada High School history. Beasley taught for many years and had a passion and the drive to make a difference. "I still like what I'm doing. I stay in contact with my students," Beasley states glowingly. Wow!

For me personally the spirit and generosity of Bud Beasley was amazing. When I started interviewing him he did not know me from Adam, but we soon developed a wonderful relationship. He was open to me as you can tell about what you just read. He allowed me into his house, allowed me to borrow several of his scrapbooks and his 1948 Reno Silver Sox uniform. He made time for me...even though he kept up a very hectic schedule even in his last years. I had a difficult time returning his uniform I eventually did. I called him a few weeks after I had given it back, we talked and he said if the uniform meant that much to me that I could have it. That is just the kind of man that Dr. Beasley was. Kind!

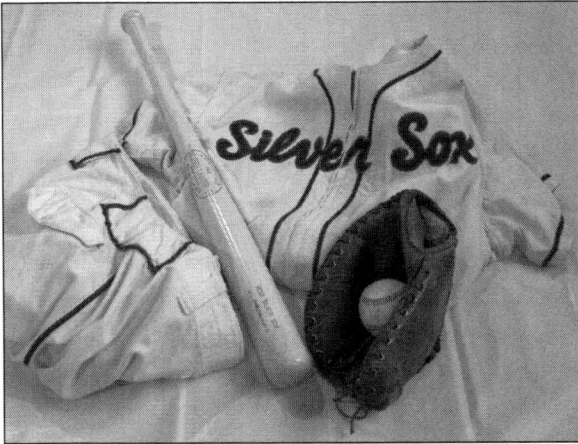

Bud Beasley's uniform, photo by Charlie Johnston

I don't know how many people Beasley has impacted in Northern Nevada. I do, however, know of one sportswriter and fan who has been touched by Dr. Beasley—me! Dr. Bud Beasley is one of the greatest people in Nevada baseball history. From the classroom to the ball field, and everywhere in between, Beasley has made a positive contribution to Northern Nevada.

Bud Beasley with Tim Mueller
(Courtesy: Sue Mueller)

3rd Inning: Reno Silver Sox/Padres

The Reno Silver Sox were a minor league baseball club affiliated with many different baseball franchises. The team enjoyed a long and very fruitful existence. The Silver Sox started out playing in the Sunset League from 1947 to 1949, then the Far West League from 1950 to 1951 and then played in the California League from 1955 to 1992. The team had affiliations with the Brooklyn Dodgers, Los Angeles Dodgers, Pittsburgh Pirates, Cleveland Indians, Minnesota Twins, San Diego Padres and Oakland A's. Only briefly did the team name change from Reno Silver Sox that was in 1982 when the team was affiliated with the San Diego Padres.

I revisited the stadium in February of 1996, a few years past its prime, the place was akin to a "Pandora's Box" of memories. Moana needed a lot of tender loving care. Paint was peeling off the seats, water was six inches deep in the dugouts, and the Sportsman's Corner scoreboard had been out of service for a few years. As I wandered around this "ghost town of baseball," the scene worsened; the press box had been vandalized, the place was abandoned and it felt like a war zone. There was not a soul to be found either "dead or alive." Moana Stadium had lost its place in society and was now lonely, quiet and filled with solitude. The only ones making memories here were the occasional seagull.

Moana Stadium was sitting on real estate that was unsure of its future. A few years earlier, the city had built a fire station that consumed a large portion of the parking lot. In addition, the Reno City Council was considering constructing a street extension through the field. I think the stadium may have survived because of a downturn in the local economy and an outcry from local youth sports leagues that said it was important to preserve Moana as a public-use facility. In reality, I believe that Moana Stadium survived because it was already built; it is hard to demolish a local sports stadium that had as many unique memories as this one.

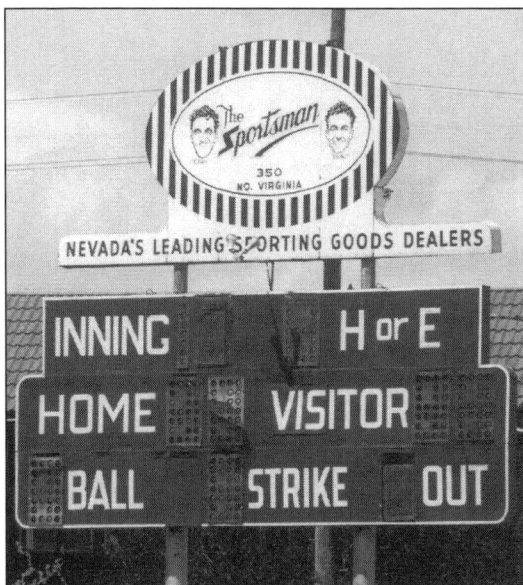

Moana Stadium Scoreboard
(Taken by Author)

The complete list of teams that played at Moana Stadium "Home of the Silver Sox" (Sources: 1991 Reno Silver Sox Program and Author's Research) follows:

Years	Team Name/Affiliate	League
1947-1949	Reno Silver Sox (Independent)	Sunset
1950-1951	Reno Silver Sox (Independent)	Far West
1952-1954	No Team	
1955	Reno Silver Sox (Independent)	California
1956-1957	Reno Silver Sox (Brooklyn)	California
1958-1962	Reno Silver Sox (Los Angeles)	California
1963 to 1964	Reno Silver Sox (Pittsburgh)	California
1965	No Team	
1966-1974	Reno Silver Sox (Cleveland)	California
1975	Reno Silver Sox (Minnesota)	California

Years	Teams/Affiliate	League
1976	Reno Silver Sox (Minn. /SD)	California
1977 -1981	Reno Silver Sox (San Diego)	California
1982-1987	Reno Padres	California
1988-1991	Reno Silver Sox (Independent)	California
1992	Reno Silver Sox (Oakland)	California
1996-1998	Reno Chukars (Independent)	Western
1999	Reno Blackjacks (Independent)	Western

It was through these memories and experiences that I started the journey of writing this book. I contacted the late Rollan Melton, a newspaper columnist for the Reno Gazette-Journal. He offered to print my request for information in his column on July 20, 1998. It was through this initial notice that I began receiving phone calls and setting up interviews as well as conducting research. Without Mr. Melton's willingness to help me this project would not have been possible.

I remember many different types of promotional days. One vivid example was free horn day. They handed out long brown plastic horns I used mine for quite some time (much to my dad's dismay). I also remember ice cream day, hot dog day, cap day, baseball card day. The horn though was my favorite. I remember looking through the fence watching games when I did not have enough money to attend games. I looked quickly through the Reno Evening Gazette each afternoon before delivering papers on my paper route. If I read about or heard about offers for free tickets I would go wherever I needed to pick up free tickets around town. I would just show up at different businesses to get the tickets. I did not buy whatever the business was selling. I always said "thank you" and the owner/clerk would appreciate my politeness.

I never had a bad experience at Moana Stadium. It was all good. It was a simple place with wooden bleachers, a broken scoreboard and only a couple of restroom stalls. The food was not that good, but that did not matter it was a fun place to experience baseball and to learn about the game…

Another extremely enjoyable part of the experience was getting autographs. After passing through the turnstile, I usually started with buying a scorecard. On it I would mark off the best players according to their stats. I always checked out the visiting roster first as I knew they would only be in town for a few days. This thrill of the chase was often more fun than watching the game itself. I soon learned that I could also ask players for their broken bats. As the game progressed and bats would get broken I would make a note on my scorecard and ask the appropriate player after the game for their bat.

My most memorable 'broken bat experience' was when I asked Marc Newfield for his broken bat. Since he was a top prospect of the Seattle Mariners at the time, I asked him to autograph it. He obliged and I have kept the bat to this day. I have not kept the bat because of its monetary value but rather the sentimental value. I know you might be thinking why does he keep something that really has no tangible cost…sometimes the memories are what counts. The memories are huge I hope you enjoy some of them from the Reno Silver Sox era.

The number of players passing through "The Biggest Little City in the World" has been equally amazing, Roberto Alomar, Bobby Cox, Dennis Eckersley, Ray Fosse, John Kruk, Kevin McReynolds and Benito Santiago, just to name a few. This list does not mention the visiting players that played at Reno's Moana Stadium. Some of the most prominent visiting players I remember seeing were: Kirby Puckett, Will Clark and Mike Piazza.

Reno's Moana Stadium is the most historic ballpark in Nevada. No other yard even comes close. The players, coaches and fans that have watched or played games are too numerous to list. I will now talk about some of the Silver Sox players that called Reno's Moana Stadium home over the years:

Emil W. "Bill" Wickert has been involved with baseball since 1934 when he was a batboy (known then as a mascot). Wickert played on the Reno Silver Sox in 1941 and 1942 and on the Reno Garage team in 1942. At the time, the Reno Silver Sox was an amateur team and Reno Garage was a semi-pro team that played at Threlkel Park in Reno from the late 1920's through 1950. Wickert made stops during his baseball career in Reno, Redding, Orland, Klamath Falls, and Medford. Earl Sheely of the Boston Red Sox drafted him in 1940. He worked with the New York Yankees as their business manager in 1946. Mr. Wickert served as President of the California League from 1976 to 1981. From the tone of Wickert's voice, his fondest baseball memory was that it was in Reno where he got his chance to play pro baseball. According to Wickert, Jack Threlkel, owner of the Reno Garage (previously located at the intersection of First and Center Streets in Reno) wanted the best team in town, and recruited players from as far away as the bay area to play on his Reno Garage team. "Threlkel recruited me right off the Reno Silver Sox team; in those days, team loyalty ran a lot deeper than it does now," Wickert remembers in a solemn voice.

While Wickert was serving as the President of the California League he recalled that "(Former) Nevada Governor Mike O'Callaghan was a huge fan of baseball". Governor O'Callaghan would host players at the Governor's Mansion in Carson City for dinner. O'Callaghan had met a prospect of the California Angels named Julio Cruz who was playing on the Salinas club during a Reno Silver Sox home stand and knew that Cruz was a base stealing threat. At a governor's conference in Boston, O'Callaghan had an opportunity to watch a game at Fenway Park and the Angels were playing. Julio Cruz came into the game and O'Callaghan told his fellow governors "this guy is going to run and steal a few bases". The fellow governors were sure that O'Callaghan was wrong, but Cruz stole 2nd and 3rd. O'Callaghan was so happy to report the good news that he called Wickert, who was in the California League office in Berkeley, California.

Bobby Cox, the current manager of the Atlanta Braves got his professional baseball career started playing in the infield for the Reno Silver Sox in 1960. As I am typing this some 49 years later, I realize that a lot has happened in the career of Mr. Cox since then. He is one of the best managers in Major League baseball history. He has an all time managerial record of 2,327wins against 1,854 loses in his 26 seasons. He currently ranks 4th all time in number of wins. The following stats are from the first season that Mr. Cox played professional baseball in Reno.

Bobby Cox's Stats from 1960 Season

Year	Club	Avg.	Games	Runs	Hits	HR	RBI
1960	Reno	0.255	125	99	112	13	75

Mr. Cox has accomplished something that no other National League Manager has ever done and that is to win 100 games over five seasons. In fact, only three other American League managers have ever duplicated the feat: Joe McCarthy (New York Yankees), Connie Mack (Philadelphia Athletics) and Earl Weaver (Baltimore Orioles.)

Ray Fosse played on the Reno Silver Sox in 1966 the team was affiliated with the Cleveland Indians at the time. It was his first season of professional baseball meaning it was the first time he got paid. "It was so much fun, being a kid and playing in Reno, not being able to get into the local establishments. I remember great meals. I remember going into the Primmadonna Casino for the 99 cent breakfast. I went to the Mapes. I was overwhelmed I was from Iowa and now was living in *The Biggest Little City in the World,*" Fosse reminisced. Maybe the best part of his assignment to Reno is that Ray Fosse met his wife.

Fosse remembers Reno playing in the California League which was a bus league. "I remember driving up highway 99 and getting a little homesick when I smelled the fresh cut hay. The bus ride was something you had to do. I did not want to pass up the opportunity to play in the Major Leagues," Fosse recalled. Fosse played the entire 1966 season in Reno and felt like he should have been called up to the Major Leagues sooner, in hindsight Fosse said, "Playing in one place (Reno) for the whole season was one of the best things that happened to me in my Major League career."

Fosse was a great player on the 1966 Reno Silver Sox team, "I remember playing in a 23 inning game against the Lodi Dodgers the game started at 8 p.m. and finished at 2 a.m. I then caught 12 innings the following night. I caught for 35 hours over two days. My season ended the next game as I suffered heat exhaustion," Fosse recalled.

Another interesting event happened in Lodi when Bo Bolinski was playing and actress Mamie Van Doren was in town watching the Lodi Dodgers play. "She threw out the first pitch and the park was packed," Fosse recalled.

The pay was small in those days as it is today a mere $800 per month. That was not much money after taxes and rent. Fosse remembers that the game was different in those days, "We had one player Ed Bayes who was 27 or 28. The clubs did not have as many players. The team was made up of a mixture of veterans and young players."

Moana Stadium had small clubhouses and was "a typical minor league ballpark" according to Fosse. "I remember the screen behind home plate was still in fair territory. I made an out on a ball that hit off the screen and then bounced into my glove."

"On the last day of the 1966 season in Reno, a lady gave me a silver dollar and she said keep this and you will never be broke. I'll never forget that. I think I still have the silver dollar. Reno is a great city and was a great place to play baseball," Fosse reminisced about his 1966 season playing baseball in Reno.

Keith Roman was one of the surprises of my research I met him one day unexpectedly at Kinko's in Carson City. I learned that he was the same Mr. Roman who worked for the Douglas County School District for many years. We got to talking and I told him I was writing a book about baseball in Nevada and he told me that he had a story for me.

During the mid 1950's Keith had been the Clubhouse man for the Reno Silver Sox. He cleaned uniforms, socks and cleats for fifty cents every two weeks from each player. Keith made about $25.00 a month from doing this.

This was during the time when Ray Perry was the manager of the club. "Ray would stick up for me. He showed me how to clean and straighten cleats. He was a very tough manager. He had a good temperament with the ballplayers. Ray would play 3rd base and pitch when needed," Roman remembered.

Tim Flannery is the third base coach for the San Francisco Giants. Flannery shares his baseball ties to Nevada with his boss,

Bruce Bochy. Flannery played in Reno in 1978 and served as the Las Vegas Stars head coach in 1995. Flannery remembers Reno with a sparkle in his eye as a great place to play baseball. "I loved Reno and the California League. Little cities are great! They are intimate places; players don't know it yet—that (baseball) is a business. Nobody is tainted, and all the players are trying to showcase their ability," Flannery reminisced.

John Kruk I did not have the chance to talk with former Major Leaguer and current sportscaster. I had the opportunity to talk with Hall of Fame 3rd baseman Mike Schmidt about John Kruk. Schmidt was teammates with one of the most personable players in Nevada history John Kruk, who also played professional baseball in Reno and Las Vegas. "Kruk was one the best hitters in the league; he was a fun guy, not too serious; he could kid around; I respected him as a hitter."

Mike O'Callaghan a fan's fan

The late Mike O'Callaghan was the governor of Nevada from 1971 to 1979. He was a great fan of the game of baseball. O'Callaghan and his wife would often make sandwiches and take them to the Reno Silver Sox when they played home games at Moana Stadium, usually on Sundays when they played double headers. On several occasions, they would host players at the Governor's Mansion in Carson City. Some of these players included Bruce Bochy, Dennis Eckersley, Tim Flannery and Del Crandel.

O'Callaghan's personal favorite baseball memories were watching his son hit a grand slam in little league and watching the final game that Mickey Mantle played at Oakland.

Governor Mike O'Callaghan and the Reno Silver Sox c. 1976
(Courtesy of the Nevada State Library and Archives)

Prior to moving to Reno I never knew what the minor leagues were. I had grown up in Southern California where the majors were king. I listened to the Hall of Fame broadcaster Mr. Vin Skully. I did not even know about the different levels of baseball let alone where Reno was and for that matter Moana Stadium. I had not even seen a scorecard or even thought about keeping score. I had not even asked for an autograph prior to moving to Reno in 1975. You could say that I did not start to learn about the nuances of baseball until living in Nevada. I was a fan who knew very little about the sport that I would grow to love.

4th Inning: People of Baseball in Nevada

One of the things that I have enjoyed the most about this project has been the people that I have met along my journey. At the conclusion of each interview I would ask if there was anyone else that I should interview; more often than not I would get a list of three or four names and phone numbers. I was amazed how one lead would lead to another. I have met people from many walks of life and all had one thing in common: the fabric of baseball. The following section showcases my interviews of Robert "Buzz" Knudson, Lyle Overbay, Mike Maddux and Ty Cobb (the writer), as well as my research about Ty Cobb (the player). The goal of this section is to give you a taste of the information that I have collected, and also to show how the game of baseball has touched so many people in Nevada.

I started out my search for interview subjects by talking with the late Rollan Melton, Reno Gazette Journal columnist. He gave me the names of some people that he thought I should contact. In addition, he made mention of my quest in a column that he wrote three times a week, and from those initial leads the interviews rolled in. And I mean rolled in, to-date I have interviewed over 125 people.

One of the first interview sessions that I had was with Dr. Bud Beasley. Dr. Beasley treated me as a member of his own family. He let me borrow his vast collection of scrapbooks and even gave me his 1948 Silver Sox uniform. I learned about not only his personality but also the great experiences he had while playing in city leagues, the Pacific Coast League and the senior circuit. He took me under his wing and gave me more contacts and helped me to get a handle on the history and lore of this great game. I learned how this famous teacher had a tremendous impact on the game of baseball.

In my research, I learned some unexpected and amazing facts. For example, an Oscar winner once played baseball in both Reno and Las Vegas. Robert "Buzz" Knudson played in Nevada during the 1948 and 1949 seasons. This in itself was not the most interesting part

37

of his life. That would come after he got married and decided to work in the motion picture industry. He worked on sound mixing crews and earned seven nominations for Academy Awards, winning three.

Through luck and gumption, I gained access to Major League figures. I attended my first spring training game in Arizona during the 2003 campaign. Hoping to interview Lyle Overbay, who played at the University of Nevada, Reno, from 1996 to 1999, I made my way into the press box and talked with the Arizona Diamondbacks staff. They told me I would have an opportunity to interview Overbay when he came out of the game. I went into the press box when Overbay was taken out of the game in the sixth inning. The Diamondbacks media rep told me he would grant me the interview soon. I had to make the transition from fan to journalist, so I took those few minutes and got my thoughts together in my notebook. Soon I got the signal, a hand-wave gesture from the Diamondbacks staff. I felt as though I had made the club … my adrenaline was really flowing now, and I was the only one granted early access to the locker room! As I made my way down to the locker room, I felt like a celebrity of sorts. Kids were waiting patiently for autographs, and I walked by, waved at Luis Gonzalez, and walked into the locker room for a great interview with Overbay.

Sometimes I learned a lot more than I had planned. For example, I went into the interview with Mike Maddux with no real expectations. I just had hoped to learn more about his background. I came away with a lot more than that. I learned some about what makes a pitcher a pitcher and some of the physical and mental aspects that go into playing the game at the Major League level. Mr. Maddux was patient and allowed me time. I had requested 20 minutes, and he gave me over an hour. I was impressed by his willingness to change his normal routine to accommodate me. I enjoyed just watching batting practice, listening to the stories of players and coaches, jokes, and just soaking up the atmosphere in the dugout.

Other times, I felt more like a detective, a "Sherlock Holmes" of sorts, like when I was hunting for clues about the great Ty Cobb (player). I went from office to office, from contact to contact, and made phone call after phone call. I felt like I was a member of the IRS trying to find somebody who owed back taxes. I was able to learn bit by bit and put the puzzle together, and what I learned was astonishing.

I hope you'll enjoy learning about the great players and coaches and others who make Nevada's baseball history such a rich one as much as I enjoyed searching and finding and meeting them.

Robert "Buzz" Knudson
From Ballplayer to Oscar Winner

I found Robert "Buzz" Knudson to be very open and honest, and candid with me. He was born in Los Angeles, California, in 1925 and graduated from Fairfax High School (LA). He played on the 1948 Las Vegas Wranglers (Sunset League) baseball team. He had a pitching record of 9 wins and 8 losses when he was traded to the Reno Silver Sox. The Wranglers likely regretted this decision, because he finished the 1948 season with a record of 20 wins against 9 losses. He played on the 1949 Reno Silver Sox squad as well. Knudson then played on the Idaho Falls team in 1951 and the Salt Lake City team in 1952. According to former California League Commissioner Bill Wickert, Knudson was one of the first pitchers to throw the slider.

"Buzz" remembered Las Vegas as "a great town, although it only had two clubs, and was all desert." He also remembered a funny story in which he and a few other teammates would eat at the Chuck Wagon Buffet, and they would "line their pockets with food and feed the rest of the team with the food."

Buzz also recalled a casino manager named "Sundown" Wells who would allow the players to play cards. They would bet $1, and when they won around $5 or $6, which was enough for meal money, "Sundown" would kick them out. "Wells was a great guy," recalled Buzz.

After arriving in Reno, he quickly became friends with Lilo Marcucci, the Silver Sox catcher. In 1949, Marcucci became the team's manager. This relationship lasted a lifetime, with visits occurring at least once a year. Buzz and Marcucci were roommates at the Old Senator Hotel in downtown Reno in 1948. In 1949 they roomed with an older lady, who lived near the Truckee River. Buzz admitted, "I love Reno." He remembered Reno's Moana Stadium as a pitcher's ballpark, "It was a strong pitcher's ballpark; the wind was always blowing against us." The stadium was later reconstructed due to a fire in 1961, and home plate was moved from the southeast corner of the park to the southwest corner. Moana has since become a "hitter's haven."

Team travel in those days was often quite difficult and at times very tiring. In 1948 the Las Vegas team used a stretched Lincoln, and the Reno teams had the services of an old school bus, which was "often uncomfortable and impossible to sleep on," as Buzz remembered. On one road trip to Southern California during the 1948 season, the Reno team bus had some problems near the town of Bridgeport, California. The team got off the bus and checked it out. Once everything appeared okay, everyone got back on. Then a few miles out of town, "a wheel fell off the bus," Buzz recalled laughing. Such was the life of a baseball player in the late 1940s.

While the baseball career of Buzz Knudson is interesting in itself, the more amazing and fascinating part of his life would soon follow. He spent 40 years working on some of Hollywood's biggest and best motion pictures. Buzz started working for the RCA Sound Company in 1952 and retired with the Todd AO Company in 1990. He did sound mixing on over 40 movies during his amazing post-baseball career. He has been nominated for seven Academy Awards and has won three, for Cabaret in 1972, The Exorcist in 1973 and E.T., the Extra-Terrestrial in 1982. Wow! How many former baseball players can say that?

Robert "Buzz" Knudson with his three Oscars (Courtesy Knudson Family)

Knudson's Hollywood studio was hired by actor Robert Redford to record the last two reels (15 minutes) of the movie The Natural. Knudson remembers that "Redford went goofy when he heard I had played pro ball." Buzz was very happy to make sure that the movie was correct in its depiction of baseball. He provided input on the way that Redford held the bat and how he stood in the batter's box. It was really more of a consultant arrangement, and Redford appreciated the input that Buzz provided.

Lyle Overbay

Lyle Overbay played high school baseball in Centralia, Washington, got recruited to play on the University of Nevada and played on the Wolf Pack squad from 1996 to 1999, compiling a .358 batting average. Overbay was runner-up for the 1999 Big West Conference MVP. He was drafted by the Arizona Diamondbacks and won the Pioneer League MVP in 1999. He has played in the Majors since 2003 playing for the Arizona Diamondbacks, Milwaukee Brewers and Toronto Blue Jays.

Lyle Overbay in 1999, Tim Mueller Photo

Overbay described his best memory of playing baseball at Nevada as "fun … Regionals were great, as the competition and environment were awesome." Overbay enjoyed the sense of accomplishment he got by playing hard every day. He shared a mutual respect with Nevada Coach Powers. Overbay stated that Powers "is a good prepared coach, who makes great calls and is always focused and ready for the game." According to Overbay, Coach Powers was a coach who would "do anything for you, he was very helpful."

I had interviewed Overbay three times before (two in Reno and one at Stanford), and I had the wonderful opportunity to interview him once again during spring training in March 2003, when I was lucky enough to get a press credential at Tucson's Electric Park. Overbay was trying to make the Arizona Diamondbacks. Even as he was about to make the big leagues, he was very cordial and kind to grant me the interview.

Overbay is very humble and thankful that he was able to play at the University of Nevada. He considers the decision to play at Nevada "as one of the best decisions I ever made." He has a very good way to keep things in perspective: "It is important to keep learning and making adjustments."

It was very obvious that Overbay was having the time of his life at Spring Training 2003. He was in a kind of dream world. "I grew up watching these players; now I'm next to them. Am I really here? I could not help but think of my own childhood and dreaming that I would one day be a Major Leaguer." This dream was about to come true for Lyle Overbay. I asked him about his relationship with Mark Grace. Overbay was very thankful to have the three-time All Star as his mentor. "He is very helpful showing me the little things, doing little things right. He has been there and done that. He helps me to find the little things that I don't notice. It is very exciting to learn," Overbay stated.

Lyle Overbay's Stats

Years	Avg.	Games	Runs	Hits	HR's	RBI's
2001-2008	0.270	852	391	824	86	393

The Maddux Brothers and Las Vegas

Mike Maddux is currently the pitching coach of the Texas Rangers. Both Mike and brother Greg have played in the Majors. Mike played for 15 seasons. Greg has played for 22 seasons and has earned 355 career victories. I am sure that Greg has a guaranteed ticket to baseball's hallowed shrine, the Hall of Fame in Cooperstown, New York. They have been the best baseball-playing tandem ever to come out of the State of Nevada.

I had wanted to interview the Maddux brothers for a long time. They spent a considerable amount of their lives growing up in Las Vegas. I was able to interview Mike Maddux at the Hubert H. Humphrey Metrodome in Minneapolis, Minnesota, in June of 2003, and I did not waste the chance.

The Maddux family moved to Las Vegas in 1976. Their dad was on active duty with the Air Force and was assigned to Nellis Air Force Base. Mike Maddux was a sophomore at Rancho High School at the time. He had played youth baseball in Spain. Soon after moving to Las Vegas, a retired baseball scout by the name of Ralph Meder saw a lot of potential in the Maddux brothers and invited them to workout sessions at Hadland Park in Las Vegas.

Ralph Meder worked with the Cincinnati Reds organization. He also worked a lot with Mike Morgan, who pitched 15 seasons in the Majors.

The Hadland Park workouts would consist of pickup games, and as Mike Maddux remembered, "Ralph would take off from where dad left off." Maddux's dad was a fast-pitch softball pitcher and was very good.

Maddux graduated from Rancho High School in 1979 and opted to attend the University of Texas at El Paso, where he played baseball for three years before being drafted by the Philadelphia Phillies in the fifth round of the 1982 draft.

Prior to our interview, the only background I knew came secondhand from watching him pitch on television. I remember the commentators often saying how resourceful he was, and how he oftentimes came to spring training with an outside chance of making the team. Somehow he always found a way to get onto a team. How did he do this? Was it by luck or circumstance? Did he just have really good connections? Or did it boil down to just doing his homework? I remember one announcer saying that Maddux had the uncanny ability to find a spot on a roster. But the results were astounding and the facts are clear: Mike Maddux pitched in the Majors for 15 seasons.

My initial thoughts were that he accomplished so much through pure, unbridled desire. I had seen firsthand how competitive and driven Mike Maddux, the pitching coach, is. He arrives at the stadium early so that he has time for a personal workout. He is a tremendous example of what it takes to have a strong work ethic, and the saying "It is important to practice what you preach" is accurate. It does not surprise me in the least that he has enjoyed a long, successful career in the Major Leagues.

The Major Leagues are a place where dreams are made. Once a player has made it to "The Show," it is the ultimate pinnacle of a baseball player's career. Reminiscing about his first start at Philadelphia's Veterans Stadium, Maddux said, "The Vet was huge; I was scared to death. For your whole life you want to get there [Major Leagues], and when you do, you feel overwhelmed."

Maddux played in the Major Leagues for 15 seasons for the Philadelphia Phillies, Los Angeles Dodgers, San Diego Padres, New York Mets, Pittsburgh Pirates, Boston Red Sox, Seattle Mariners, Montreal Expos and Houston Astros. A summary of his stats follows.

Mike Maddux's Career Stats

Years	W-L	ERA	Games	Saves	IP	BB	SO
1986-2000	39-37	4.05	472	20	861.2	284	564

Maddux really enjoyed his time in the Major Leagues. "The adrenaline flow when you are pitching in the Majors does not compare with anything else," Maddux explained from the visitor's dugout at the Metrodome in Minneapolis. While he reminisced, his eyes sparkled and his voice was one of a very happy man.

He was named the pitching coach of the Milwaukee Brewers on November 2, 2002. Mike summarized coaching by saying, "It's the little things that add up, like executing; communication is the key. If everyone overachieves, that helps the team."

Spring Training 2003 was an interesting time, as that was the first time Maddux the player had become Maddux the Major League pitching coach. It was challenging to fit everyone into the rotation. Twenty-seven pitchers reported to spring training. Starters needed to be scheduled for 25 innings of work each, and relievers needed 12 innings of work. Maddux stressed the importance of having a plan as a coach, but also the importance of being flexible and creative. "If you write something down, make sure it is in pencil," he commented.

Seeing the improvement of the players on a daily basis is what makes the coaching experience worthwhile. "The players should take something with them every day," Maddux said. In a "perfect world," a starting pitcher would throw 50 pitches before the game, between 12 and 15 pitches each inning and eight between innings, for a total of 230 pitches for a complete game. A typical box score only gives pitchers credit for their "official pitches" that are thrown to batters, over the course of a game, which is usually in the 100 to 120 pitch range.

The routine for a Major League pitching coach is demanding. The following chart summarizes the routine on the afternoon that I met Mike Maddux.

Mike Maddux's Personal Routine
(for a 6 p.m. Game)

Noon	Arrive at the ballpark Personal workout Eat lunch
2:00	Throw batting practice
3:00	Soft toss getting the starter loose
4:00	Figure out how to pitch to opposing team
5:20	Meet with starting pitcher

The most interesting comment that Maddux told me was the following: "If we [coaches] had the knowledge that we do now, we all would be Hall of Famers. If upcoming players simply pay attention and learn to do what they are told, they have a better chance at becoming a Major League player and, maybe more importantly, enjoying a long career in The Show". Maddux was willing to share what separates a short-term and a long-term player: "Having a strong work ethic and having a plan are important." This advice is also extremely important to young players.

Several people have had a huge influence on the career of Mike Maddux. First, his brother Greg: "Greg helped me with the mental approach of the game." Second, "Tony Gwynn taught me how to counter hitters, watch the hitters' feet [caster or short to ball]. And third, Felipe Alou taught me how to have a pitchers' meeting and how to communicate in a straightforward manner."

"Making it to the big leagues is the easy part; making it a career is the tough part," according to Mike Maddux. He has definitely made it a career. Thanks, Mike, for allowing me to learn a little about the art of pitching.

Greg Maddux's Career Stats

Years	W/L	ERA	Games	Innings	BB	SO
1986-2008	355-227	3.16	744	5,008	999	3,371

Greg Maddux played his high school baseball at Valley High School in Las Vegas coached by Rodger Fairless. Coach Fairless said, "Our relationship is good; we talk in the off-season." Fairless continued, "If I was a kid, Greg Maddux would be my hero. He's a great role model. He is a team player. He is not selfish. He should be an idol."

The accolades continue for Maddux. Tony Gwynn, elected to the Baseball Hall of Fame in 2007, said the following about Greg Maddux, "He might be the best pitcher today. He is consistent and has great location. His ball moves a lot. He is very competitive. He is one of the best pitchers due to his thinking ability." San Francisco Giants manager Bruce Bochy said, "Maddux is the best pitcher of the last 10 years." Former Major League manager Buck Showalter said, "Maddux gets respect from a far. He gives his team a chance (to win) every time he pitches. He is a baseball player that happens to be a player. He enjoys taking on the responsibility of his team without having a problem with it."

Rollie Fingers was elected to the Baseball Hall of Fame in 1992 as a pitcher and I felt like he was very well qualified to talk with about Greg Maddux. "Maddux has learned to pitch very well. He moves the ball in and out. He is not overpowering. He has a good sinker. You think from the neck up", Fingers said. Fingers was a thinking pitcher as well, so he relates very well with the way that Maddux approaches the game.

Thanks Tony and Rollie for talking with me about Greg Maddux who will be joining you soon in Cooperstown, New York in baseball's hallowed shrine the Hall of Fame.

Two Cobbs, One Nevada

Nevada has a very rich baseball tradition when it comes to the last name of Cobb. Tyrus Raymond Cobb, the famous American League baseball player, and Ty Cobb, the famous Nevada sportswriter, have both called Northern Nevada home.

Tyrus Raymond Cobb, the baseball player, played for the Detroit Tigers and Philadelphia Athletics from 1905 to 1928. He led the American League in hitting 12 times and retired with 4,191 Major League hits. In 1936, Ty Cobb was in the first group of baseball players elected to the Baseball Hall of Fame in Cooperstown, New York.

Ty Cobb was a baseball player of huge stature. He was a fiery competitor with a mean streak. Part of his game plan was to "mess with your mind." Cobb often distracted pitchers and other players when he got on base. His goal was to glean an extra step or two so that stealing the next base would be easier. He would also distract the pitcher with a mean look at every opportunity.

Ty Cobb established over 80 records in his Major League career. He had many nicknames, including "The Georgia Peach," "Tyrus the Terrible" and "Phantom Mercury." Most baseball players only have one nickname, but since Cobb earned three, perhaps that means Ty Cobb was the greatest baseball player ever.

Cobb was often known for his temper both as a player and in retirement after baseball. After he moved to Nevada, he got into scuffles in a Reno casino, a Carson City restaurant and a Virginia City bar. Cobb was always the toughest man around and never lost a fight, either in Virginia City or at the stadium. The "Georgia Peach" was one of baseball's most colorful personalities.

For several years of his retirement, Cobb lived at a lodge at beautiful Glenbrook, Nevada. Glenbrook is located on the east shore of Lake Tahoe. He enjoyed the serenity and quietness of the lake he enjoyed relaxing. Mr. Cobb did so much thinking at Glenbrook; one must wonder what he thought about. Did he think about the future? Did he think about the game of baseball that he had played at an amazing level? Or did he simply try to relax and enjoy the serene beauty of Lake Tahoe?

I submit that he pondered many questions. Since he was a huge star of baseball and a wealthy man, he didn't have to worry about his next meal. He did have to worry about thieves who could break into his hunting lodge when he went on trips. He would still study and invest in the stock market. Ty Cobb seemed to be a man who could readily communicate about things that he knew a lot about, like baseball and the stock market.   This might have been because of his love of hunting and fishing. He lived in a 10-room hunting lodge in beautiful and very private and secluded Glenbrook. He loved his hunting dogs with a passion. He took great pains to train his dogs, and always made sure that they were well taken care of when he left his home. He would often take vast amounts of time and make plans to go hunting in a new location. He immensely enjoyed hunting and camping with his friends.

Ty Cobb was more than "just a great ballplayer"; he was a masterful and resourceful businessman as well. He purchased stock, and often called his stockbrokers before he went to the ballpark. He freely gave investing advice to his friends and teammates. He purchased several hundred shares of Coca Cola stock many years before it became popular to do so. As if stocks were not enough of a gamble for Cobb, he also enjoyed casino gambling. There is report of him winning $12,000 at the famous Riverside Hotel and Casino in Reno.

Ty Cobb, the Great Nevada Sportswriter

What is just as amazing is that Nevada had yet another Ty Cobb! The second Ty Cobb was a sportswriter for the Nevada State Journal from 1938 to 1960. Ty Cobb the sportswriter was named after Tyrus Raymond Cobb, the baseball player. Their lives would be linked forever through name and geography.

I had the opportunity to interview Ty Cobb the sportswriter before his death in 1997. I found Cobb the writer to be a very kind, gentle and caring man, not to mention extremely sharp and witty. His first love was sports. When I interviewed him he told me about the first Reno professional team in 1947. He was speaking with a heart that knew that baseball was more to Reno than just baseball; that team was a link to the outside world. The nearest Far West League team that year was Las Vegas. Cobb reminded me that "Reno contributed many players to the Major Leagues."

We talked for a spell about his brilliant 22-year career with the Nevada State Journal, one of two Reno daily newspapers along with the Reno Evening Gazette. Cobb's eyes sparkled when he spoke about the time he spent behind the public address microphone at Moana Stadium. He acted as though this was one of his favorite things in life. I think that Cobb would have enjoyed working as the public address announcer full time, if the income had been sufficient to provide for his family. However, that was "not in the cards" for Ty Cobb, and he lived his life in a manner in which he had no regrets.

We then talked about the teams and the players that Cobb saw at Moana Stadium. He told me that his favorite all-time Reno team was the 1955 Reno Silver Sox as they turned an amazing four triple plays. Cobb continued by stating that "Willie Davis may have been one of the best players to come out of Reno." Cobb seemed awestruck remembering that one of the best all-time Major League relief pitchers, Dennis Eckersley, played in Reno in the 1972 and 1973 seasons. Eckersley was elected to baseball's hallowed shrine, the Hall of Fame in 2003.

Cobb spoke about fond memories of the old Negro League teams that played games in Reno in the 1920s and 1930s. He said, "The Kansas City Monarchs and the House of David teams really packed [the fans into] Moana Stadium." Cobb said that the great Olympic track star Jesse Owens once raced against a horse at Moana Stadium; Owens won!

We talked about unusual games, and one of Cobb's favorite games was played in the late 1950s, in which Steve Dobkowski of the Visalia Oaks walked 20 batters and at the same time struck out 20. In that same game, Cobb said, "Herb Knowles hit a grand slam to win the game for Reno." The following list is sportswriter Ty Cobb's Reno All-Star Team*:

Ty Cobb's All Time Reno Silver Sox Team

Designated Hitter	Fran Boniar
Pinch Hitter	Lillio Marucci
First Base	Dick Nen
Second Base	Duane Kuiper
Shortstop	Charley Smith
Third Base	Ken McMullen
Left Field	Guy Richards
Center Field	Willie Davis
Right Field	Jose Vidal
Catcher	Butch Wynegar
Pinch Runner	Tom "Hotfoot" Humber
Pitchers	Al Corwin, Dennis Eckersley, Dick Tidrow, Jim Kern, Ed Farmer, Pete Richert and Bill Singer
Relief Pitcher	"Rapid" Robert Arrighi
Manager	Ray Perry
Coaches	Roy Smalley, Tom Saffel and Harry Warner
Umpires	Doug Harvey and Bob Engel

*Source Cobbwebs, p. 109

Cobb made sure that he was complete and accurate with his all-star list. I was surprised to learn that many of these people played professional baseball in Reno.

Since Ty Cobb the sportswriter was born in Virginia City, Nevada, in 1915, he had a strong love of the Comstock Region. He reflected that sentiment in a Cobbwebs story he wrote about Virginia City's old Pan Mill baseball diamond: "Even though there was no grass, ground rules were made necessary by the physical conditions and that few ballparks in the world had such terrain." He continued to write about the Pan Mill diamond with warm affection: "A young

Italian who lived nearby made himself a good piece of change by uncovering lost baseballs and selling them back to the home club."

Cobb even had his hand on the "business of baseball" before Minor League Baseball was a real business. He told me that the Sportsman's Corner Sporting Goods Store had a 99-year lease on the Moana Stadium scoreboard. Talk about a great business move; I wonder how many fans have come through Moana Stadium since the Sportsman's logo has been a mainstay of the scoreboard ... I bet that Chet and Link Piazzo (owners of the Sportsman) are very happy indeed that they signed the agreement for the scoreboard.

Cobb seemed to have a clear vision for sports and how to make it readable. He wrote with a passion that was unmatched at the Nevada State Journal (1938 to 1960). He enjoyed writing so much that he continued to write a weekly column, "Cobbwebs," until near his death in 1997.

Ty Cobb the Nevada sportswriter found that his life seemed "linked" to the baseball players' life. At birth, he was named after the great baseball player. As an adult, he received the baseball player's divorce papers by mistake, which, as he wrote in a column, "was quite a surprise to my wife." (Sept.7, 1985, RGJ). There was even a "Ty Cobb" night at Moana Stadium in Reno. On this night, three Cobbs were present at Moana Stadium: Ty Cobb the baseball player, Ty Cobb the sportswriter, and Ty Cobb the sportswriter's son. There was plenty of "Cobb" for everyone in the stands.

The relationship was also a social one, where each Cobb would visit the other at home. The sportswriter would often get mail, bills and lost Ty Cobb items sent to his home address. The baseball player Cobb never listed his phone number or address in the telephone directory, but the writer's number was. So the contact would be made with the writer, and he would relay the message.

Ty Cobb the baseball player and Ty Cobb the sportswriter had a huge influence on Nevada history — one as a lifetime resident and the other as a colorful retiree. Nevada history is awesome, if we take the time to look "under the covers."

Nevada is proud that Ty Cobb the sportswriter lived, worked and called Nevada his home. He was a champion of sports reporting and a true gentleman. You are missed Mr. Cobb, Nevada's all-time best sportswriter!

5th Inning: Bobby Dolan Baseball Dinner

The University of Nevada baseball team hosts an annual fundraising dinner. This event started in 1985 and has had some of the biggest names in baseball attend and speak about the grand game of baseball. When you go through the list it is a very impressive list of names. The very first speaker was Tommy Lasorda he spoke for the first two years and then teamed up with former manager Roger Craig in 1990. Tommy then came back to speak at the 2009 dinner I had the opportunity to ask the question of why is this dinner so important to Tommy Lasorda. Mr. Lasorda said, "I wish you could have had an opportunity to play with him. "He was a guy who played his heart out. He didn't have the ability a lot of guys had, but he played...as hard as he could with the ability God gave him. He and I and Sparky Anderson, the three of us were very, very close." Tommy Lasorda said at the 2009 Bobby Dolan Dinner. I figured that it was a special relationship but I had no idea how special it was. To hear it from the living baseball legend Mr. Tommy Lasorda who was only a foot or so away from me was amazing. It was...well was pretty surreal to say the least.

Tim Mueller with Tommy Lasorda, 2009 Dinner

Bobby Dolan played from 1952 to 1960 in the Los Angeles Dodger organization (minor leagues). Bobby was offered the chance to play at the major league level, but he was not feeling well and declined the offer and Maury Wills was called up instead. Dolan retired from organized baseball in 1960 to attend to his growing family. Bobby was a very well liked and charismatic man. While playing in the Minor Leagues, Dolan met some very famous baseball people including eventual Los Angeles Dodger manager Tommy Lasorda. Through those connections Bobby was able to start an annual fundraising dinner for the University of Nevada baseball team. After Bobby's death in 1990 the dinner was renamed in his honor, the Bobby Dolan Baseball Dinner.

What is amazing about Bobby Dolan is not how much talent he had but his drive and his love of the game. I learned that Bobby was great friends with Tommy Lasorda and Sparky Anderson. According to Tommy Lasorda, "Bobby had heart and I loved him." This is very high praise from the famous former Los Angeles Dodger manager.

I have had the opportunity to attend the dinner four times in 1998 (Reggie Jackson), 2000 (Paul Molitor), 2004 (Tommy John) and 2009 (Tommy Lasorda). This list is impressive but when you look at the complete list it is even more so. This list represents 13 Hall of Famers, 28 World Series champions, many All Star games, and countless home runs.

I am somewhat mesmerized by the fact that the so many World Series players have spoken at the Annual Bobby Dolan Dinner. Think about this for a moment. Willie Mays was a member of the 1954 World Series Champion New York Giants, Whitey Ford played on eight championship teams for the New York Yankees, and many many others. It is incredible to me and shows how important this dinner is to former major league players.

It is incredible that all of these speakers spoke in Reno for a benefit for the University of Nevada baseball team. Here is the impressive list!!

University of Nevada Bobby Dolan Dinner Speakers

Year	Speaker	Year	Speaker
1985	Tommy Lasorda	1997	Earl Weaver
1986	Tommy Lasorda	1998	Reggie Jackson*
1987	Roger Craig	1999	Joe Morgan
1988	Roger Craig	2000	Paul Molitor*
1989	Sparky Anderson	2001	Frank Robinson
1990	Tommy Lasorda Roger Craig	2002	Dusty Baker
1991	Willie Mays	2003	Whitey Ford
1992	Don Zimmer Mark Grace	2004	Tommy John*
1993	Brooks Robinson	2005	Jon Miller
1994	Johnny Bench	2006	Goose Gossage
1995	Willie Stargell	2007	Will Clark
1996	Pete Rose	2008	MikeKrukow Duane Kuiper
		2009	Tommy Lasorda*

*attended by author

In 1998 I was able to hear Reggie Jackson speak. This was my first Bobby Dolan dinner and I enjoyed listening to Mr. Jackson talk about his experiences and how he became to be known as Mr. October. It was fun and exciting he did an excellent job in speaking.

In 2000, I had the opportunity to attend my second Bobby Dolan Baseball dinner. At the dinner, I was able to talk with former Major Leaguer, Paul Molitor, the guest speaker. I had a great time watching the interaction between the University of Nevada baseball players and Paul Molitor who was elected to the Baseball Hall of Fame in 2003. I was even able to have my photograph taken with "Molly." I enjoyed watching how Molly interacted with the players. He was like a dad, a dad talking about how to hit the ball. He was enjoying his role as a guest and spending time with the players. It was a lot of fun to watch.

Paul Molitor with Tim Mueller, 2000 Dinner

In 2004, I was able to listen to Tommy John speak. Again he did an excellent job speaking.

But by far the best speaker of this group was Tommy Lasorda who I heard speak on February 3, 2009. Tommy was able to get the crowd into his speech. He was able to be funny at will. He did not look like he was even working hard at speaking. He seemed like he was a natural. He was happy, sad even at times a little mad. But one thing was certain and that was he represents something bigger than the team he works for he represents baseball!

At times he told stories about various Dodger players at spring training. He talked about the World Series. He even spoke briefly about his friendship with the late Ronald Reagan, the 40th President of the United States.

I was captivated by his every word and I know that I was not alone. He was vivid and crisp and he drew us all in. I am very thankful that he and Bobby Dolan had been friends and not just friends but very good friends. It was a blast!!

6th Inning: University of Nevada

My history with the University of Nevada begins with Jackie Jensen who was the head baseball coach of the Nevada Wolf Pack baseball team for only two seasons—1970 and 1971. His impact came from what he had done some 20 years prior. Jensen played in the major leagues from 1950 to 1959, and again in 1961. Mr. Jensen played on the New York Yankees, Washington Senators and Boston Red Sox. In 1958, Jensen won the American League MVP Award, hitting .286 with 35 homeruns and 122 runs batted in.   He was inducted into the Boston Red Sox Hall of Fame on May 18, 2000. The Boston Red Sox enjoy a rich baseball history that few other teams can match. It was very interesting to me that someone so famous at the major league level chose to be a part of Nevada Baseball History.

Jackie Jensen, Joe DiMaggio and Mickey Mantle
Source: National Baseball Hall of Fame Library, Cooperstown, NY

Jackie Jensen at Yankee Stadium
Source: National Baseball Hall of Fame Library, Cooperstown, NY

Mr. Jensen was a true gentleman in every sense of the word. In his book, former long-time Reno Gazette Journal Columnist Rollan Melton wrote, "Baseball star Jackie Jensen was a classy gentleman who volunteered his time to help young people. He retired to Reno and became the baseball coach at the University of Nevada[1]."

William Peccole was a Nevada Alumni who was also a tremendous benefactor to the University of Nevada baseball program. Peccole donated a total of $700,000 to the construction of the baseball facility that bears his name. A plaque at the ballpark reads:

---

[1] Page 104, *Sonny's Story: A Journalists Memoir*, Rollan Melton, University of Nevada Reno Oral History Program, 1999

"A special thank you to Bill Peccole for his generosity and kindness and to athletic director Chris Ault, whose vision and determination brought baseball back to our campus with the construction of: William Peccole Park....a testament to the Peccole Family."

> *Signed,*
> *Wolf Pack Baseball Fans*

As a thank you to the family the University placed this ad in the Reno Gazette Journal.

> We Love Baseball,
> Hot Dogs,
> Apple Pie And
> William and Wanda
> Peccole.

In my opinion it is safe to say that the University of Nevada baseball team simply would not have one of the top collegiate baseball facilities in the nation without the financial contributions of the Peccole family. Thanks so much!!

The University of Nevada has a rich and illustrious athletic heritage. I first began to understand and appreciate this history during the 1992 baseball season when I attended my first college baseball game. This peaked in both the 1999 and 2000 seasons as Nevada reached the NCAA Baseball Regionals both years, and I was able to attend both series at Stanford University in Palo Alto, California. I had a great time. Following are my notes, ideas, thoughts, feelings and observations. I hope you enjoy them as much as I did!!

1999 Stanford Regional

It was great to be a member of the media at the 1999 Stanford Regionals. I was able to go many places that the fan was not able to go. For instance, I was able to go down onto the field, into the bullpen areas, to the news conference area, and I was able to sit in an assigned seat and eat and drink on Stanford's dime. It was a wonderful experience all the way around. Eating, sleeping, watching even the drive to Palo Alto was cool...and I couldn't wait to go back.

"Good Vibrations" and "409" songs were playing on the loud speakers. For me it was a combination of factors that made this first game feel like a championship game the crowd was excited, people were happy to be there, it was post-season excitement. The University of Nevada baseball team seemed confident, friendly and calm. They seemed like they had some unfinished business to deal with and that was to beat Stanford at their own yard.

I talked with Coach Powers before the game and wished him good luck. I was also able to reintroduce myself to Dan Gustin, former radio announcer for the Wolf Pack. Gustin remembered me and that felt great. I really felt like I had begun my journey as a more serious maybe somewhat well-connected fan. I did not even know that I would be attending this series until a couple of days prior. I was in a groove and even felt like I could put on a uniform and play on the team.

The first game pitted the University of Nevada against the University of North Carolina. UNR has about 200 fans and UNC only had about ten. I was surprised by this, as UNC has many alumni and I thought that there could be quite a few UNC alumni living close to Stanford's Sunken Diamond.   As I looked around the Sunken Diamond, I was surprised how beautiful the park is. It has a very well maintained lawn; trees surround the entire ball park. The scoreboard is large. And the sound system is as close to perfect as I have ever heard it was clear and the volume was right. In addition, the stadium employees are kind and eager to help in any way possible. I was very surprised to learn that the Pac 10 conference does not allow beer sales. The foul areas are extremely large; I estimate that half of the outfield would equal the sum of the foul areas. I can now see why Stanford pitchers often have such great seasons. The seats do not have backs (chalk one up to Peccole).

As Nevada head coach Gary Powers and North Carolina's head coach Mike Fox exchanged lineup cards I felt like a member of the team. I felt like I was standing with them in this ceremony of extreme politeness. I envisioned everybody talking in formal, upbeat, cordial and calm voices. I imagined that everyone was using "Mr." greetings.

Nevada started Chad Qualls and Carolina countered with Mike Bynum. Both pitchers threw great games, Qualls struck out 10 and Bynum struck out 12. Both allowed four runs. The game was won with one mighty swing of the bat. North Carolina third baseman, #32 (I will never forget that number) Ryan Earey, hit a three run homer in the top of the 12th. You could hear a huge sigh come out of the Nevada Wolf Pack dugout as the ball shot like a rocket over the leftfield fence. I think that home run ball may have made it all the way to Reno, if not physically, for sure the "ting" sound was heard in Reno. This game had a little bit of everything, great pitching, sound defense, very similar coaches, and each team had the same number of hits (lucky number 13). Unfortunately, for the University of Nevada it did not equal a win. Nevada lost the first game to Carolina by a final score of 8 to 5.

When a team loses the first game of a double elimination tournament in 12 innings, their spirits are crushed. At the postgame news conference it was very easy to see the hurt and disappointment. It was easy to hear as well. Lyle Overbay, the superstar right-fielder from the University of Nevada was one who was still upbeat and optimistic at the conference. He went 2 for 6 for the game. There was a twinkle in his eye, which seemed to be a sign that the team would be ready to play Saturday.

I wondered what adjustments will be made. What did Nevada Coach Gary Powers tell his team after losing a game that they could have won? We would have to wait until tomorrow to find out. Oh the joys of baseball...

1999 Stanford Regional Game 2
Nevada vs. Loyola Marymount   May 29, 1999

As I made my way into Stanford's Sunken Diamond I shook hands with a future NFL Hall of Famer, Jerry Rice who was out for a morning jog. I wanted to talk to him but the only word that could come out of my mouth was "Hi." This got my adrenaline flowing early and quickly.

On Day 2, the Pack must win at least the first game to prolong their season. They face a team that lost its first game to Stanford the night before. The team is the Loyola Marymount University (LMU) Lions and there is a Nevada connection—former Nevada Assistant Baseball Coach, Jason Gill, now coaches on the LMU squad. I wonder how much of an advantage it is to have a coach on your team that knows how and what the other head coach is thinking.

Coach Powers reminded me that following this formula is crucial to a team's success at a Regional Tournament:

"FUNDAMENTALS LEAD TO FOCUS, WHICH EQUALS SUCCESS."

Can the Pack bake a win? I didn't know, but I was very cold. The field crew had just turned on the lights for an 11:00 am start. Where were we anyway, in Alaska? I couldn't get warm, and I had to get up and walk around many times just to get thawed out.

This game was nip and tuck. LMU took the early lead in the second inning leading 2 to 0. Nevada Catcher Matt Ortiz got the first run for Nevada across in the third inning. LMU answered in the bottom of the inning. Sensing that the game may slip away, Coach Powers made the call to the bullpen, and Luke "The Count" Drakulich charged in from the bullpen. He pitched five and two thirds innings, allowing no runs on five hits. This was his longest outing of the year and it couldn't have come at a better time.

Nevada continued to trail in the game, 3 to 2, until the ninth inning. Justin Martin, the speedy Nevada second baseman, Joe Inglett and Matt Ortiz were due up after they were done Nevada led the game by a score of 4 to 3 and held on for the victory.

I had the opportunity to interview Jason Gill after the game... I felt it would be great to make the Nevada connection, so I did. Jason said that he enjoyed the opportunity that he had at Nevada. He said that Coach Powers gave him control to make decisions. He said "Coach Powers is a winner, he doesn't expect anything else, he is a great motivator and he has great practices." Jason Gill also paid the Nevada Baseball fans a huge tribute by saying that the "fan support is tremendous in Reno."

As I mentioned, I was so cold that I needed to drive back to my motel in Sunnyvale and don some more clothes. I put on everything I had—t-shirts, polo shirts, a flannel shirt and my jacket. I also packed my ski cap and gloves. I never needed the cap but I did wear the gloves for the next game. I turned the car radio to 103.7—a cool Bay Area jazz station. I knew I needed to take a little time out to warm up before heading back to the stadium. So I drove north on US 101 past Stanford and turned off in San Mateo. I filled up my tank at AM/PM and drove around a little more. On my way back I tuned to 90.1, the home of Stanford Sports. To my amazement North Carolina was beating Stanford 4 to 2; UNC only needed three more outs to beat Stanford. The roof then fell in on Carolina, Stanford scored five runs in the top of the ninth including three on John Gall's three-run game-winning home run. I was shocked. The fans then bounced to their feet and clapped in unison. I then understood the mystique of Stanford baseball.

North Carolina would now have to rebound quickly to face a rested Nevada squad. Would this meeting end with the same results of the Friday night meeting, with North Carolina punching out Nevada? In between games, I was pondering whether or not Nevada would have enough energy left to beat Carolina. I wrote down my thoughts "I feel as though Nevada will win no matter who we play."

1999 Stanford Regional Game 3
Nevada vs. North Carolina   May 29, 1999

I continued to write before the game started. My head was full of a myriad of thoughts and I could feel the emotional roller coaster that often mirrors sports. I also had a difficult time gauging if the players were tired.

It did not take long to get my answer. In the bottom of the first inning Matt Ortiz again hit a sac fly to score Justin Martin from third. It was the first time that Nevada had led in a Regional game this year. Nevada tacked on two more runs in the third. Nevada was well on their way to play Stanford on Sunday. Matt Rainer, Nevada's starting pitcher, kept getting stronger as the game went on. He only allowed one run in the fourth inning. He threw an incredible number of pitches—146 in all. He lifted his team in a big way. This strong outing allowed Nevada to eliminate North Carolina by a final score of 5 to 1. The stage was now set for what many Nevada fans, including me had wanted to see earlier—a showdown between the University of Nevada and Stanford University.

During the post-game news conference Coach Powers said "That was a real big win for us. It's been a long day, we've been here since 9:00 this morning and we showed a lot of character." Winning Nevada pitcher Matt Rainer was modest in his assessment of the game, "I have a few things to improve on; I had too many walks."

Today I really started to see that the University of Nevada baseball team of 1999 was made up of a lot of players that all worked hard and worked together to reach the common goal of the championship game against Stanford. Nevada's big boppers, Lyle Overbay and Don Price, were not carrying this team on their backs. The other players were lifting up the team and breathing life into an emotionally tired team. These players were Joe Inglett, Justin Martin, Matt Ortiz, and Matt Rainer. It is awesome when a team pulls together in a way that it normally does not. Each player stepped up to the plate and seemed to think "carpe diem" because they acted as if they wanted to "seize the day". This Nevada team was unselfish and was able to find a way to win even when they had "their backs to the wall." The spirit of the Nevada baseball team was beyond description.

For the first time in my life I watched three innings of baseball on the field and what I noticed most was the confidence and attitude of the Nevada players and coaches. I also enjoyed watching the great defense and the speed that Justin Martin used at second base to gobble up every ball hit his way. Lyle Overbay was starting to flex his defensive muscle as well. He fired many cannon-like throws in to hold base runners to singles.

I drove back to my motel room in Sunnyvale and had a hard time relaxing. I had many thoughts and images from the day continue to pop up in my head. I took a shower thinking this would allow me to relax. It didn't. I then watched the news. That didn't work either. Finally, I sat down and jotted down a few thoughts...

Since I have not been to a College World Series game, I am enjoying the ambiance, spirit and formality of the Regionals. I experience the emotional swing within a baseball game for the first time as 'an insider' and saw this swing as enormous. Nevada's emotional state went from being at a -

*10 on Friday night, after the loss to North Carolina to a +100 after
eliminating both North Carolina and Loyola Marymount on Saturday.*

And finally I admitted to myself I was tired and was able to
plunge into a deep sleep.

1999 Stanford Regional Game 4
Nevada vs. Stanford   May 30, 1999

I decided today that I would spend the whole game standing
or sitting on a chair on the actual baseball field. My thinking was that
this would either be the last game of a great 1999 season or game one
of a great "Championship Sunday." I got onto the field early, as I
knew that space would be at a premium. I felt a little like an animal
trying to mark my territory early and often. I left my briefcase as my
calling card on the chair. The weather was hot and sunny. I should
have worn shorts, I thought. Oh well! I started to get light headed
before the game started and had to run up and eat something in a
hurry 15 minutes before game time.

I will now tell you what I was thinking before the first pitch of
the Nevada/Stanford game...Nevada seems confident, happy and
eager to play. In the two head-to-head meetings, Nevada won the first
game in Reno by a 7 to 5 score before dropping the second at Stanford
by a final of 16 to 14. Since both games were close, and Nevada had a
chance to win today, I thought this game would be a gem. The
University of Nevada team was relaxed. During warm-ups, Joe
Inglett did a flip in front of the dugout, and Justin Martin and Lyle
Overbay were playing catch. Lyle Overbay was rocking out listening
to the stadium music. The game was ready to begin and it would be
very exciting to see if the Wolf Pack could beat the Cardinal!

Nevada was sent down quietly in the first. The Cardinal came
up and put up a confident run in the bottom of the first. This was in
sharp contrast to the Nevada/North Carolina game in which Nevada
scored first and went on to breeze through the game. In the top of the
fourth, the Nevada bats started to heat up and Nevada led 2 to 1. This
lead was short lived, as Stanford scored three times in the bottom of
the inning. I started to think that Stanford was just too strong and

confident at this time. And I was right, when in the sixth inning; the Cardinals chalked up three more runs and were leading 7 to 2. Nevada would score two more runs, but it was too little, too late and that was the end of their outstanding season. The Nevada team played with the heart and soul of few teams.

Post Regional thoughts written June 10, 1999

Although the Nevada baseball season has been over for almost two weeks now, the season has not ended for me.

I am following the NCAA Regional tournament, and two 1999 Nevada foes have made it to the College World Series (CWS) in Omaha, Nebraska. The two teams are the Stanford Cardinals and the California State Fullerton Titans. Ironically, these two teams will match up in the first round of the CWS. I wonder if Coach Powers is scratching his head wondering if Nevada had beaten Stanford in the first round of the Regional, would they be playing Cal State Fullerton? I would bet Stanford's "farm" on it. Coaches think about all of the nuances of the game. 'What if I had done that?' or 'what if that player had made that play?' I think Powers would like to be in the position to knock one of these great baseball programs out of the CWS. Am I thinking revenge? I don't think so...I am thinking about sportsmanship, competition and the joy of victory. That is the great part of writing I can write whatever I want.

Let's dream for a moment;

The place: Omaha, Nebraska.

The stadium: Rosenblatt Stadium.

The occasion: 2010 College World Series.

The fans: 25,000.

The opening round matchup pits Big West Conference runner-up Nevada vs. Fullerton. In head-to-head matchups this season, Fullerton beat Nevada all three games. Revenge is very sweet when it comes to playing baseball in Omaha at the CWS. Oops! I slipped. Did I say 'revenge'? I meant sportsmanship.

Could you imagine the post game excitement to beat Fullerton in the first round? But the story gets better...

Nevada plays the Florida State/Texas A & M winner. And Wham! Nevada beats them too! Hmmm…let's see what happens next? Fullerton wins their game and has to play Nevada again. Matt Rainer pitches a nine inning gem like he did against the North Carolina Tar Heels back at Stanford. Lyle "Over the Bay" Overbay hits a grand slam, Justin Martin steals three bases, and Don Price adds a two run homer. The Pack eliminates Fullerton…Woof!!!

Now remember, the CWS is not over, but for Nevada the "dragon has been slain." They feel like David in the Bible story of David and Goliath. And Nevada has just beaten the pants off Goliath (Fullerton).

2000 Stanford Regional

The University of Nevada had an exciting season in 2000. It seemed as if the Wolf Pack was in a great position to make the move to the Western Athletic Conference. The Pack finished in a tie for first place in their final season in the baseball-rich Big West Conference, with a conference record of 21-9. For the second consecutive year, the Nevada Wolf Pack was awarded a regional berth to play at Stanford University.

The Wolf Pack ended the season with an overall record of 38-19. However, their record did not do the team justice. For the first time in Wolf Pack baseball history, the team possessed all three tools that are needed to build a top quality collegiate program: pitching, fielding and (a Nevada staple) hitting. In the 1990's, Nevada had built a strong tradition of boasting some of the biggest and brightest offensive players in the NCAA. Led by Joe Inglett in 2000, Lyle Overbay in 1999, Corky Miller in 1998, Justin Martin in 1997 and Andy Dominique in 1996, the Wolf Pack has had a steady stream of offensive weapons.

Inglett had a tremendous senior season in 2000, hitting .435 with 10 home runs, and 48 runs batted in. For his heroics, Inglett won Big West Conference Player of the Year honors. He finished his Nevada career with a .384 average, 19 home runs and 179 runs batted in. He played a host of positions for the Wolf Pack in his four year career including second base, shortstop, third base, catcher and outfield. Maybe his biggest accomplishment was his leadership.

Being a silent leader, Inglett allowed his attitude and work ethic do the talking for him. He raised his batting average every year that he played at Nevada. Joe Inglett had nothing but praise to say about his career at Nevada, "Words can't explain it....it has been a wonderful ride. I could not ask for more. I have had great support. (The) crowds at Peccole are awesome. They are always hollering and backing us. Coach Powers is a great man. He taught me how to be a man, how to handle adversity and how to play hard. (On draft hopes) I would like the opportunity to play....it doesn't matter where." Joe Inglett got drafted in the 8th round of the 2000 Amateur Draft by the Cleveland Indians.

Ryan Church finished his Nevada career in fine fashion as well. Church finished his senior campaign by hitting a robust .382 driving in 62 and hitting 14 home runs. "I remember being a freshman and having other players take me under their wings; I'm very thankful to them. The Peccole fans are always backing us and trying to rattle the other team. Coach Powers has been like a father to me. He taught me how to be competitive, how to live life, and how to be a man. He pushes you and I am very thankful to him. I had great teammates like Dominique, Overbay, Corky, Brink and Jay Ulman—they were good (friends) on and off the field. (On the draft) I have been contacted by 10 or 11 teams and will wait for the call." Church was drafted in the 14th round by the Cleveland Indians.

Matt Ortiz finished an outstanding career at Nevada by batting .377 with 15 home runs. Ortiz recalled on Senior Day, "I am happy with the time I spent in Reno. I have graduated from baseball with a great group. Our seniors have played well very solid. All of the seniors lead in different ways, some by example, others by talking, and others with instruction." Matt had the opportunity to lead the team from the important position of position that of being the catcher.

Don Price had the unique opportunity to play collegiate baseball in his hometown. Price finished his senior year hitting .343 and knocking 17 homers. "Nevada made me a great offer; they had a good program in a good conference with a difficult schedule and good competition. Coach Powers is a feisty coach, he never quits and he has really good focus. He (Powers) gets the best out of people. It was nice to stay at home with my friends. I had a good experience at Nevada with no regrets," Price stated.

What made the 2000 season different is how the Pack had the whole package, including pitching led by senior Chad Qualls (11-4, 3.88 era) and freshman sensation Darrell Rasner (14-2, 3.52 era.)

Although only a freshman on paper, Rasner rose far above that status in his initial season. He performed like a seasoned veteran. "I have had a great time at Nevada. We have a great program. We always have Regional hopes. It is an honor to play Stanford. I have a better curve ball here," Rasner states about his season. He had a better curve with the humidity reacting to the flight of the baseball from his hand to the catcher's mitt. It will be very exciting to follow the progress of this great pitcher. I think he may become the first Wolf Pack player to be drafted in the first round of the 2002 Amateur Baseball Draft. I was right he was drafted by the Montreal Expos.

Chad Qualls became only the third Nevada Wolf Pack player to be drafted in the second round, joining Rob Richie and Chris Singleton. He was drafted by the Houston Astros.

Once again, I was afforded the great opportunity to attend the Stanford Regional in Palo Alto, California. It was Memorial Day weekend, May 26 to 28, 2000. There was a very strong field; the host Stanford Cardinal, the Alabama Crimson Tide, Fresno State Bulldogs and Nevada Wolf Pack.

I had attended the tournament the year prior and felt like a rookie, so I was better prepared in 2000. I knew what my main purpose was: to conduct player and coach interviews. I even tried hard to nab an interview of Stanford's elusive Jason Van Meetren, who had attended Bishop Gorman High School. I tried and I tried, but could not find out of his whereabouts. Seems pretty strange, doesn't it? I probably gave this "chase" too much of my energy. I thought it was cool that a player from Las Vegas could be playing against the Wolf Pack. I was curious: were there any connections that could be made? Had he played against Darrel Rasner in a high school tournament? I had more questions than answers. I conducted many more interviews than I did the prior year and even had a little time to socialize at Stanford's Sunken Diamond. If you have never had the pleasure of watching a baseball game at Stanford's yard, I would strongly recommend it.

Everything from the ticket takers and greeters at the gate, to the public address announcer, to the perfectly manicured playing surface, to the beautiful backdrop of Stanford University—it all creates an image and feeling of a professional stadium.

I first interviewed Fresno State Bulldog head baseball coach Bob Bennett. I was able to learn that he and former UNLV head coach Fred Dallimore had a great relationship. I felt like coach Bennett was teaching me something and I really enjoyed it. I can see how he has been the head baseball coach at Fresno State for the past 32 years. This Bennett-Dallimore relationship surprised me in a pleasant way. I also asked Coach Bennett about Nevada head baseball coach Gary Powers. "He has done a very good job at Reno. He has brought Reno up to a power level and has (really) picked up the program," Bennett said. Coach Bennett surprised me by talking with me about how the head coaches often have a relationship with one another off the baseball diamond. I found him to be candid, polite and to the point. It was a joy to interview Coach Bennett.

I then interviewed Stanford head baseball coach Mark Marquess. Of Fred Dallimore, he said, "Coach Dallimore established a program (at UNLV). He is well respected and was always well prepared for the games we played." Of Gary Powers, Coach Marquess answered, "I have a lot of respect for Nevada coach Gary Powers. He is consistent. We play (Nevada) because they are tough." These were great quotes from another great coach, Mark Marquess.

Player Interviews

Justin Martin played at the University of Nevada from 1996 to 1999. He was drafted by the Pittsburgh Pirates in the 1999 Amateur Baseball Draft. The interview was conducted via phone on February 29, 2000, just before Martin left for spring training. I really enjoyed talking with Justin Martin and he was very easy to talk with and it felt like we were friends after our conversation. I wished him the best of luck in spring training.

We talked about his reflections playing for the Nevada Wolf Pack. We talked about snow falling on the field and shoveling snow off the field. Part of the Wolf Pack's home field advantage is due to the extreme weather conditions in Northern Nevada. Justin Martin remembered having a difficult time getting adequate practice time on the field and about having to play baseball inside the gym as the field was often covered with snow. Martin said, "Nevada has loyal fans, win or lose." Justin said that "Coach Powers requires hard work and is building Nevada into a power house program." When it's time to go on road trips, the Nevada Baseball team travels in class, wearing a suit and tie. "We have a first class organization at Nevada," Martin said.

"Coach Powers was almost like a father figure to me; he gave me guidance. He helped me to make the adjustments to college life and taught me how to take responsibility (for my life)", Martin said. During his first year, it was difficult for Martin to wake up and to be at the 6 a.m. workout sessions.

"Sometimes players come and go, and it's hard to be a student athlete," Martin admitted. "Nevada Baseball teaches you a lot about life, not just baseball," Martin states. Playing in the Minor Leagues was a totally different ballgame for Justin Martin. "First you have the responsibilities of travel. You need to save money, pay bills and have to learn to work well with other players. There is a lot to learn," Martin recalls. "There is no homework in the Minors, and you take care of business. There is also the adjustment to make playing with wooden bats," Martin said.

Darrell Rasner Jr. played at the University of Nevada, Reno from 2000 to 2002. He played high school baseball at Carson High where he lettered all four years. Rasner described Coach Ron McNutt as "a good coach who was very helpful both in baseball and life." Rasner really enjoyed his time at the University of Nevada, "Nevada has a great program, and I have had a good time pitching there."

Darrell Rasner, Jr. in Little League
Courtesy: Rasner Family

Darrell got drafted in the 2nd round of the 2002 Major League Draft by the Montreal Expos (46th pick overall); he felt many different emotions when I interviewed him three days after the draft. Rasner thought that the draft was a "big process." He felt like there was a lot more to it than most people would recognize. Rasner felt excited, honored, and very fortunate to have good coaches and strong family support. He felt like it was a tremendous honor to just be considered for the draft, and to be selected to play professional baseball was a huge opportunity. His first stop was in Vermont to play for the Vermont Expos of the New York-Penn League. "I'm looking forward to the learning experience, finding out what is new and how things work," Rasner said about his future. He is looking forward to pitching to wooden bats, "Pitchers are rewarded for marking good pitches when wooden bats are used—breaking a bat is a reward and there are fewer bloopers," Darrell did not hesitate when he responded to what he is looking forward to the most—playing big league baseball. He couldn't wait, and he did not have to wait long!

I asked Darrell about what advice he would give to someone who is playing high school baseball and he said, "Work at battling through adversity; this builds character. It's hard but remember that your teammates will support you."

In closing, it was a wonderful opportunity for me to talk with a local player that just got drafted (and one who is very well poised to make it to the major leagues). Darrell ended the interview by saying, "Being drafted is a dream. It's unreal. It's exciting for me and my family." Good luck, Darrell. We hope you pitch in the major leagues for many years to come.

Coach Interviews

Coach Gary Powers graduated from Douglas High School in 1966, earned his undergraduate degree in 1971 and Master's degree in 1972 from the University of Nevada Reno. Powers was a starting pitcher at the University of Nevada for the 1970 and 1971 seasons. He began his coaching career at Incline High School (NV) in 1973. He then coached at Wooster High School from 1977 to 1981 and then accepted his first collegiate head coaching job at Shasta College (in Redding, California.) He accepted the head coaching job at the University of Nevada in 1983 and has been there ever since.

When Coach Powers began coaching at the University of Nevada, the team shared the facilities of Moana Stadium. Maybe a better way to describe this would be that they 'tried to share'. Coach Powers remembers a lot of bickering between the different groups involved with the ownership and upkeep of Moana. "It was a frustrating situation as we didn't know from one day to the next when our practice time would be. It was almost impossible to field a college program from Moana Stadium", Coach Powers recalls. The Nevada baseball program was at a real crossroads during this time. The choice was a simple: one either build a baseball field on campus or drop the baseball program all together. Coach Powers told an interesting story about the teams' struggle at Moana Stadium from the 1987 season:

"Nevada was scheduled to play a double header against Santa Clara. The Reno Padres finished their game at about 3:30 we started to go out on the field for batting practice at 3:45. There was one huge problem: the bases, including home plate, were missing. Someone from the Padres had removed the bases and locked them up. Our game was scheduled to start at 6 p.m. I had to drive up to the University get our bases and our 'dig in type' home plate, rush back to

Moana Stadium and lay out the field with tape measures. That was my worst memory of being head coach at Moana Stadium."

Coach Powers says that there are some distinct differences between Moana Stadium and Peccole Park, "At Moana the wind blows out to right field, at Peccole it blows across the field from right field to left field." The playing conditions at Peccole are much better than Moana. Peccole is much newer, with quality stadium seating, expanded restroom facilities, a well maintained playing surface. The team has more control over what is done and not done at the stadium. This has been a huge benefit for the University of Nevada baseball program.

Peccole Park was set by the NCAA Baseball Rule Book. "We wanted a good teaching environment so we could teach our players the fundamentals of baseball. Peccole Park has been a real savior for our baseball program," Coach Powers proclaimed. William Peccole, a Nevada alumnus, donated funds to make construction a reality. Since Peccole Park opened in 1988, the Nevada baseball team has won 376 games while losing only 175 (68%) within Peccole Park's 'friendly confines'.

Coach Powers described his love of the game of baseball, "If I'm not coaching, I'm watching a game. It's my life," Coach Powers states.

Coach Powers believes in a basic coaching philosophy:

"I teach baseball fundamentals to help a player to become a sound player. When ability levels even out, the player becomes consistent. I stress breaking apart segments of the game to help prepare a player to be mentally ready to play every day. Keeping focused and concentrated gives the player a distinct edge."

Coach Powers is very happy that he is coaching College Baseball. He has the job that he wants, and is fulfilled. He describes his favorite aspects of coaching, "Working with the kids allows you to see what society is like. It keeps me young at heart. I like to see people improve. I like seeing what hard work can do. I enjoy seeing how players improve not only on the field, but as people. Baseball provides us with a tool to teach players what life is all about. Both sacrifices, and teamwork, relate directly to life. (Coaching includes) helping kids through the tough times. That is what coaching is all about."

Coach Powers had a difficult time stating his favorite Nevada teams. He remembers his first year coaching the "Bad News Bears" as a rewarding experience. That team started out with only 4 players, and "I had to scramble to field a team. The team won 19 games, and they really should not have won that many. The kids really worked hard." Powers remembers fondly. Coach Gary Powers is a very humble man and this shines through when he describes his favorite players, "My favorite players are the ones that no one reads about. Nobody knows them. If you can make your worst player somebody, you always have a chance to win."

Coach Powers described two of his star players from the 1999 team (Lyle Overbay and Don Price) as "Great kids that have strong work ethics, and they have been rewarded for the jobs they have done. In addition, they have had tremendous impacts on our team."

Coach Powers had many mentors throughout his lifetime. He first mentioned his dad, the late Walter Powers. "My dad was a hard-nosed guy. (He was) a demanding coach who cared about his players."

A Nevada great had an impact on Coach Powers, "Jackie Jensen taught me a lot about baseball. I learned about coaching by not only his actions, but from the things that he did not do. I was fortunate that he taught me. I learned a lot from him. I learned that the thirtieth guy on the team is as important as the number one guy. Everyone on the team needs to be treated equally."

Gary Powers with Coach Jackie Jensen
Courtesy of University of Nevada

Coach Powers also gained from his coworkers, "Coach Sellers was great, as we both were the same type of guys. I was his defensive coordinator in football, and his was my assistant baseball coach. That was a great relationship as things just rubbed off. (Also), Former Athletic Director Chris Ault has a strong work ethic and dedication to the university. He has done a lot for the University of Nevada."

Coach Powers learned his passion early on, "I have known what I wanted to do since high school. Coach Keith Loper gave me a chance and taught me values." I think that Coach Powers is very thankful to these mentors in his life. Coach Powers has been blessed to have good people around him and by having the opportunity to develop those relationships. All of these people, including Coach Gary Powers, have been successful.

I think that the most enduring mark of any person is receiving compliments from peers in their field. Coach John Savage of UCLA, describes his relationship with Coach Powers, "He never looked over my shoulders. He trusted me. We were together for 5 years. He taught me a lot about college baseball."

Fresno State head baseball coach Bob Bennett states, "Powers has done a good job at Reno. He brought the program up to a power level. The program has grown a lot in the last 15 years."

Stanford head baseball coach Mark Marquess says, "We play Nevada because they are tough. They are very consistent and I have a lot of respect for them."

If you are reading, I would like to say, thank you Coach Powers for your dedication to baseball in Nevada!

University of Nevada Coaching Records

Name	Years	Win	Loss	Tie	%
Jackie Jenson	1970-1971	25	45		.357
Keith Loper	1972-1973	41	38		.519
Barry Mc Kinnon	1974-1979	140	154		.476
Del Youngblood	1980-1982	98	73	1	.561
Gary Powers	1983-	795	621	4	.559

7th Inning: Love of the Game

I first became a living breathing fan that had the thirst and hunger for the game of baseball after I moved to Reno, Nevada. I think this was due in large part to how close I lived to Moana Stadium; it was an easy trip to make. I typically would ride my bicycle or sometimes got dropped off by my parents. All I know is that it was always fun. In addition to Moana, there were a few other places to watch a game in Reno.

The former Manogue High School site (adjacent to UNR's Peccole Park) in Reno is another such locale. The Manogue Miners played at Victory Field (an awesome name for a ballpark!). The park used to sit in a great location adjacent to Peccole Park. With a grand view of the Sierra Nevada Mountains, it would be difficult to find a more scenic location for a ballpark than Victory Field. When I visited it on March 20, 1999, I almost froze to death. As I stood, shivering, too frigid to sit down, the snow was falling and the wind was howling. At times, it was difficult to follow the path of the baseball in the wind-blown snow. The swirling snowflakes were very distracting to the eye. Every fan had many layers of clothing on. Twenty or so "die hard or harder" fans stood in the stands, and more than that looked on from their cars, many running back and forth to keep warm. Such is the life of a baseball fan in Northern Nevada.

Going to college at the University of Nevada, Reno the closest Major League teams play in the Bay Area. I have had opportunities to watch a number of games in San Francisco. One day I was afforded a great chance to switch positions from fan to player/coach in the summer of 1999. I attended fan appreciation day at Candlestick Park in San Francisco with my good friend Jim. The date was June 27, 1999, and the time was about 2 in the afternoon. Jim and I got to the ballpark, and to my amazement saw that the outfield fence was open. I said, "Jim let's go over there and see what is going on." We went over, and I was very surprised to see fans all over the place—even walking around on the field before the game. 'Wow, was this another dream?' I thought. We could go wherever we wanted, even into the dugout! It was simply awesome to sit in the dugout. I got to sit where then-manager Dusty Baker sat, and my mind was filled with situations and plays. I imagined 'Do I throw Tony Gwynn a strike on a 2-1 count? Do I call a pitchout? Do I give Barry Bonds the green light to swing? What would I do if I still had Matt Williams on my team?'

It was the first time ever in my life in which I was able to sit in a Major League dugout, and I will not soon forget it.

We soon settled into our seats, and I began to keep score. Usually it is very difficult for me to stay focused on my scorecard for the entire game. Over the course of the game, I felt the same distractions, even some new ones—they now served garlic fries that smelled really yummy. Despite these distractions, I was able to keep my concentration, and kept score for the whole game (maybe the smell of garlic fries kept me interested in my task). I watched for any switch in momentum. The crowd soon began to chant, "Beat LA, Beat LA!" There was a huge amount of emotion at this game. It felt like a playoff game when San Francisco relief pitcher Rob Nen came in to close the game for the Giants. It was a wild crowd following the victory.

On the drive out of the ballpark, I started to reminisce that this might be my last game at Candlestick Park. The year was 1999 and rumors had circulated that the Giants may move to St. Petersburg, Florida. It is now quite amazing to look back at this time and see how well the Giants have done with their new downtown ballpark. It is now very difficult to image the Giants without their glistening ballpark on the bay. It was not known that then they would be staying in San Francisco. They did, and fans from all over are very glad that they did.

I will remember Candlestick Park for many reasons: from a rained-out Padres game, in which my car (a 1974 Pontiac Ventura) broke down near Donner Summit on the way home. I had to call my parents and my friend's parents to come and pick us up from the town of Truckee. There were more good times I experienced at Candlestick. One was a Giants vs. Expos game, in which Dennis"Oil Can" Boyd threw me a ball from second base during batting practice. Even some of the Expos, including Tim Burke, Tim Wallach and Dennis "El Presidente" Martinez, signed autographs for me. I also remember a Reds game at which I was so close to the bullpen that I could watch the pitchers warming up. I was even able to snag an overthrown ball with my trusty baseball glove. I had been frozen and cooked to perfection within the confines (I would not call them friendly for either fan or player) of Candlestick. It seemed as though it was the park that had everything.

Talking about being a fan of the game, I was a Los Angeles Dodger fan for the first part of my baseball life roughly 1974 to 1983. But that all changed on a late season day when the Dodgers said they were not going to resign Mr. Steve Garvey, my favorite player. He was signed by the nearest National League team to LA the San Diego Padres as a free agent. Since I was watching the "class A" Reno Padres a minor league affiliate play at Reno's Moana Stadium it seemed very logical to make the change. I have stayed true to my colors, but after marriage I have also become a Minnesota Twins fan as my wife is from the land of 10,000 lakes.

I got married to my beautiful wife, Sue, on December 15, 2001. What is also amazing is that I could not separate myself from baseball even for one day. I carried a baseball to church and asked our wedding photographer to take a picture of me with the ball. It was good to get married and have the connection to baseball as well. Call me crazy if you want to. I like to say that I am just a fan of the game.

Baseball...Even on my wedding day!!
Courtesy of Frederick Green

For me personally there are really only two seasons every year, baseball season and non-baseball season. Life always seems a little bit more fun after pitchers and catchers report to spring training around the middle part of February. By the same turn after the last out of the World Series life is a little bit more passé'. The diversion of baseball is a diversion that I enjoy I even talk about it for a month or so after the World Series and start talking a little bit about it before Spring Training.

Once I became a member of the Society of American Baseball Research (SABR) in 1998 I learned that I was not alone. I get a newsletter once every six weeks, a semi-annual research journal and two baseball books a year. It is cool to be connected with an organization that is trying to make the game as good as it can be. I am proud to be a member of SABR.

I also play a game called Ultimate Baseball with a group of friends. I have been playing in this league since 2001. My team, the Timville Nine, has appeared in two World Series, winning it all in 2006. This is a great time and shortens that non-baseball season.

So you could really say I don't have an off season. I am playing, reading, writing or talking baseball at all times. My Toastmasters group is amazed that I can talk at will about it; I'm not. It is, without a doubt, my sport. I don't even follow any other sport, not even from the casual perspective. I have said for quite some time that I enjoy knowing one sport well and that is the one with the 9½ inch white leather ball with red stitches. It is a game without parallel; one without an equal. It is, and always will be, America's Pastime.

7th Inning Stretch:

Wrigley Field/Yankee Stadium

Over the last two baseball seasons I have had the distinct privilege of visiting both Wrigley Field and Yankee Stadium. I consider these two of the greatest baseball shrines ever constructed along with Boston's Fenway Park. I would consider myself very fortunate to visit Fenway.

I visited Wrigley Field on August 31, 2007. I was able to visit it with the love of my life, my wife Sue, and two friends from Minneapolis. It was fun from the time that we left the hotel, even riding the subway before getting off at a place called "Wrigleyville". People were getting on and very quickly the train was full of Cubs jerseys, t-shirts and—I think the most important thing—baseball chatter and discussion. Any really good baseball town has it, I have not been to many but the ones that I have been to Chicago, New York and L.A...you hear it (if you listen or if you start a conversation). As we got off the subway train I noticed that things now had the Cubs logo, the trash cans and signs around the outside of the park. We saw people standing around a statue of the Cubs unofficial mascot, Harry Caray. People were talking really chatting to anyone and everyone who would listen and having a ball. It really seemed like a place that one could just hang out at and spend a day, season or lifetime especially if they had a radio to tune into the game. We stopped and took our picture with the statue that is larger than life, just like the late Mr. Caray.

I knew that I was in for a great afternoon when my eyes started to tear up when I walked through the turnstiles. I was very pleasantly surprised that the field was so close to the seats. I was in awe of the beauty and I got the real feeling of why they call it the "Friendly Confines." I wholeheartedly agreed. I was not in any hurry to get to my seats and I just happened to find a Nevada connection at Wrigley. His name was Chad Qualls and I had last seen him playing for the Nevada Wolf Pack at the Stanford Regionals in 2000. He was playing for the visiting Houston Astros. I was not sure at how willing this now big-leaguer would be to converse with a fan. But much to my delight, I was able to strike up a conversation with him at Wrigley Field. Wow! We talked a little about this and that. Then he went and got me a baseball and tossed it up to me. I started to tear up a little more. I asked my wife for a pen and I was able to get him to autograph it. I was captivated, and knew that I would have a hard time rooting for the hometown Cubbies today. I sat in a chair nearby and just soaked in the atmosphere that was Wrigley Field...a place like no other.

With the Chad Qualls autograph at Wrigley Field!
(Courtesy Sue Mueller)

I could only imagine what other historic ballparks would have been like...places like Ebbet's Field, Cominsky Park, the Polo Grounds and Braves Field.

I was able to visit one of those larger-than-life ballparks, Yankee Stadium, on July 19 and 20, 2008. The thoughts and experience riding the subway train were akin to that at Wrigley the summer before, with one huge exception; there were tons more people. You really felt the crunch but it was a good crunch. People of all backgrounds in a big city focused on one thing—the Yanks. Love them or hate them...26 World Series Championships, all in one stadium, is very special very special indeed. I saw a shirt that said winning 26 was not rocket science. I think it might be. No other major league team has accomplished what the Yankees have.

Walking in, I felt like an intruder trying to penetrate a concrete fort. Security was tough. There were three layers. It was impressive I wondered if I could simply be catapulted in? Where are the seats located? Could I even see the field? Many thoughts and images came to life... Yankee Stadium felt bigger than life itself. Imposing, cold, unfriendly, but still, I and 56,000 fans were clamoring for a way to get in. We got through security without much trouble.

In a stadium called the "House that Ruth Built," where the Babe, the Iron Horse, the Mick and Yogi[2] called home, I felt like I was quite near the center of the baseball universe. If this was not it I could hit it with a good throw. To me, it is simple why this place is so special—26 championships and enough great players that they could have their own Hall of Fame. Actually, they do have one. It is called Monument Park, and, for the unprepared, it is more difficult to see than the Mona Lisa. On both days, we arrived two hours before game time (when the gates opened), but we did not have any luck and were unable to get in to the line before they cut it off. I saw the monuments from a distance, but I could not get into the mini-fort within the big fort.

I watched the Yankees and A's take batting practice. I did not pay a ton of attention as I wanted to watch the stadium as much as I could. I had fun just being there...it was almost as much fun looking around and feeling the stadium as it was watching the game. I wanted to soak it all in I did, and it was great!! I will not forget the experience and am very thankful for the opportunity to see a game at Yankee Stadium[3]. Joe DiMaggio summed it up best in October 1949 when he said, "I want to thank the Good Lord for making me a Yankee."

---

[2] I would like to clarify these names: "the Babe" was George Herman (Babe) Ruth, "the Iron Horse" was Lou Gehrig, "the Mick" was Mickey Mantle and "Yogi" is Yogi Berra. The Yankees to my knowledge have the most nicknames of any baseball team.

[3] It will be very interesting to see if the Yankee mystic can carry over to the new ballpark the new Yankee Stadium that will open across the street in 2009.

8ᵗʰ Inning: Southern Nevada

Imagine Las Vegas in the 1940's it was a small desert community nothing like it is now. It was not the entertainment and convention destination that it is today. It had a population near 20,000. It was still "growing up". When the Sunset League was formed in 1947 the Las Vegas Wranglers became the first professional baseball team to play in the city. The league was comprised of teams from Anaheim, Reno, Riverside, Ontario and El Centro. A few years later, the league expanded with teams from Arizona and Mexico. Las Vegas played in the Sunset League from 1947-50.

The Wranglers played exhibition games in Boulder City and Henderson and made their debut in Las Vegas on April 14, 1947, when they concluded spring training at the New Youth Town Park in Sunrise Acres. The home opener was on April 25, 1947, around the site of the Dula Community Center. The Wranglers defeated the Reno Silver Sox, 5-2, before a crowd of 2,000.

The original Cashman Field in the new Elks Stadium was planned for the 1948 season. The Wranglers debuted at "the original" Cashman Field, which up until that time had been used for football and rodeos, on May 21, 1948. Las Vegas defeated Reno, 10-7, before a crowd of 1,515. In 1949, Las Vegas captured the Sunset League title with an 88-39 regular season record. In 1951, the Sunset League combined with the Arizona-Texas League to form a 10-team Southwest International League. Following one season, the league split again. In 1953, the Sunset League as well as the Wranglers folded.[4]

Five years later, in 1957, Las Vegas joined the Arizona-Mexico League and played one season. In 1958, the San Jose Pirates of the California League moved to the city on May 26 and the L.V. Pirates played the remainder of the season.

From 1959-82, Las Vegas was without a professional baseball team until the Spokane, Washington franchise relocated to Las Vegas to begin the 1983 Pacific Coast League season.

---

[4] www.lv51.com

Marv Einerwold played for the Las Vegas Wranglers baseball team in 1950. The Wranglers played in the Sunset League with San Bernardino, El Centro and Riverside California, Yuma, Arizona and Mexicali and Tijuana Mexico. Einerwold mostly played first base and was known as "The Mauler" as he could hit the ball regularly to 400 feet. Marv made $350 a month for playing and received $3 a day for meal money. The average salary was $300 a month so Einerwold had a very respectable game at first base.

Original Cashman Field, Las Vegas
Source: Cashman Collection/UNLV Special Collections

Einerwold was drafted into the Korean War and this ended his dreams of playing in the Major Leagues. When he returned from the war he played for part of the 1953 season but at age 23, "I was really old," Einerwold stated. "I did not make much money but played young," Einerwold said. He also played and managed the Cashman Cowboys, which played 30 to 40 games a season. The Cowboys played in the late 1950's to mid 1960's and played teams from Nellis Air Force Base, the west side of Las Vegas and Henderson. One of Marv's teammates Bob Lillis went on to play in the Major

Leagues on the Los Angeles Dodgers, St. Louis Cardinals and Houston Colt 45's/Astros from 1958 to 1967. "I made more playing semi-pro baseball than I did playing pro ball. It did not seem right but that is the way it was." Einerwold reminisced. In the late 1950's Einerwold managed the Las Vegas Colts baseball team. The Colts brought in many semi -pro and rookie teams to play in Las Vegas.

The modern era of Las Vegas professional baseball started in 1983, when the Spokane Indians of the Pacific Coast League moved to Las Vegas also nicknamed "Glitter Gulch" and changed their name to the Las Vegas Stars. The team has played since then at beautiful Cashman Field, a 9,334 seat stadium. The team has been a AAA affiliate of the San Diego Padres (1983-2000), Los Angeles Dodgers (2001-2008) and now the Toronto Blue Jays since their arrival in Las Vegas.

Cashman Baseball Field, 1983
Source: Las Vegas News Bureau/UNLV Special Collections

I had the privilege of attending a Las Vegas 51s game at Cashman Field on Tax Day of 2003. I thought, what better way to capture the memories than preparing pregame notes? I spent most of the next hour moving from section to section making an attempt to capture my personal memories from different parts of the ballpark.

I just got to the stadium and am sitting behind home plate. I would like to say there is a flurry of activity, but the only activity is me writing. If the music was not playing on the PA system, my pen would be making the most noise at Cashman. Players are stretching, playing catch, and running down the foul lines on both sides of the field. It is time for the hometown 51s to take batting practice. They are really laid back and are having fun. They are wearing blue shorts and gray t-shirts. It is difficult for me to comprehend that they are 'working' but this is what they get paid for to play a game. What a life!

(Used with Permission)

The quiet stadium now starts to explode with a multitude of sounds; the crack of bat hitting ball, ball catching leather, and rock and roll. The atmosphere feels more like spring training than the pregame routine for a Pacific Coast League game. All of these players are just one phone call away from realizing a dream. That dream to play in the Major Leagues.

As I glance around the stadium, I am engulfed in a sea of blue, yellow and orange seats. The foul lines are crisply chalked and the grass field is expertly trimmed. It is only me and the game.

When I pause and look up, I wonder who has sat in this seat– a celebrity, a politician or someone else? After all this is Las Vegas... Have they been back, if so how many times? I have such a wonderful feeling that I have the chance to watch the game I love with a passion. What better way to spend the evening?

As I ponder my life, as a baseball fan, and look back, I think it was kind of strange that I have lived in Nevada since 1975 and have never seen a professional baseball game in Las Vegas until tonight.

My mind drifted back a couple of years to the time that I was able to interview 'Mr. Padre' Tony Gwynn at an interleague game on June 7, 2000 about Las Vegas and he said, "Las Vegas knows and respects baseball."

Major League Baseball in Las Vegas

The Oakland A's were remodeling and expanding the Oakland Coliseum needed a place to open the 1996 baseball season. Well sort of. They played their first 6 games home games at Las Vegas's Cashman Field. Cashman Field accommodated the A's in a beautiful fashion. Former Oakland A's Manager Art Howe said, "I enjoy spending time in Las Vegas."

Big League Weekend

"Big League Weekend" is an annual event in Las Vegas, which showcases several major league squads in their final spring training exhibition games. I have had the opportunity to attend two of these series and I really had a great time. Vegas always rolls out the red carpet for the teams and the excitement of Las Vegas transcends to the awesome confines of Cashman Field. The City of Las Vegas is a natural baseball venue because of their weather, availability of hotel rooms and reputation as the entertainment capital of the world. There is some talk of expanding the annual Big League Weekend event to hosting spring training teams.

Former Oakland A's and UNLV pitcher TJ Mathews remarked, "Big League Weekend is fun. I saw some of my old coaches and was able to talk with them."

Former Arizona Diamondbacks player Luis Gonzales said, "Vegas is a neat place. It's exciting just going to Las Vegas. It's fun to watch spring training there. The economy is doing very well and there are many things to do."

Former Major League Manager Buck Showalter said, "I like spring training on the West Coast; there is better weather there."

The first few seasons in Las Vegas

There has been a rich history of minor league baseball in Las Vegas. This history started during the first few years that the Las Vegas Stars played. The following chart shows how this history started:

Player	Year(s) Played
Bruce Bochy	1983-84
Greg Booker	1983-84
Larry Brown	1983-84
Darren Burroughs	1984
Floyd Chiffer	1983-84
Fritz Connally	1984
Mike Couchee	1983-84
Jerry Davis	1983-84
Jerry DeSimone	1983-84
Harry Dunlop	1983
Ozzie Guillen	1984
Tony Gwynn	1983
Andy Hawkins	1983
Tom House	1983-84
Mick Kelleher	1983
Rick Lancellotti	1983-84
Joe Lansford	1983-84
Mike Martin	1983-84
Kevin McReynolds	1983
Felix Oroz	1983-84
Mario Ramirez	1983
Ron Roenicke	1984
Mark Thurmond	1983
Ron Tingley	1983
Ed Whitson	1983

Source: 1985 Las Vegas Stars Program

Influential People in Las Vegas Baseball

No discussion of minor league baseball in Las Vegas could begin without talking about Don Logan, the longtime General Manager of both the Las Vegas Stars and now the Las Vegas 51s.

Don Logan

Don Logan has been involved with Las Vegas professional baseball since 1984. Logan started out as an account executive with the Las Vegas Stars, was promoted to general manager in 1991, and finally to team president in 2000. While this is very impressive, I think that it is equally interesting to talk some about where and what Logan was doing prior to 1984.

What is very unique about Don Logan is that he was born and raised in Tonopah, Nevada, which is a scat over 200 miles north of Las Vegas. Logan graduated from Tonopah High School in 1977 and played both basketball and football, oddly enough baseball was not played at the high school. Don Logan got much of his news by listening to the radio; specifically, he listened to KMJ from Fresno, which was bounced off a radio tower in Reno. Logan remembers listening to Giants broadcasts of Willie Mays. During the summer months, Don worked construction.

Don Logan
Courtesy: Las Vegas 51s

After high school, Logan got interested in pursuing a degree in law. He started attending law school in Sacramento, California. While in Northern California, he attended some San Francisco Giants games, and soon after, came his desire to become a sports agent. Through networking, Don met Bob Lurie the former General Manager of the Giants. Don showed interest in working in the baseball industry, and Lurie encouraged him to write to all the Major League and AAA ball clubs. Bob also told Logan that it would serve him well to learn the minors.

Logan remembers his first teams as very special. "Since we all were a similar age and enjoyed playing golf, we got along well," Logan recalled with a smile. Some of these players included Larry Brown, Mike Martin and Felix Oroz.

At the time of my interview with Logan, over 1,340 games have been played at Cashman Field during Logan's tenure. I figured there had to be some unique moments. Don shared a few of those with me. "Dave Staton had a 'Bull Durham' type moment: he hit a 500' homer with only a few thousand people in the stands. Larry Bowa managed with a lot of intensity. Devon White had the most speed. He scored from first on a hit into the gap. It was special to see Mark McGwire play here as well," Logan said. I could tell that he was very happy to be able to go to work at the ballpark.

Logan also said that many celebrities go to games at Cashman Field just "to relax" among them are actors, singers and athletes.

Former and late Nevada Governor Mike O'Callaghan had the following to say about Don Logan, "He has not forgotten where he was from. He made baseball work in Las Vegas. He likes what he does and does a good job with anything that he does." Praise indeed from a class act to a class act.

The praise and admiration for Don Logan continued, "He is one the most respected operators in the Minor Leagues. I first met Logan during the winter meetings in the late 1980's," Russ Langer stated.

Jim Gemma

Jim Gemma worked at the University of Nevada, Las Vegas as the Sports Information Director for 19 seasons. He has also been the official scorer for the Las Vegas Stars and 51s for 18 seasons. In 2003, he was named the Media Relations Manager for the Las Vegas 51s. So in a word, he is the resource when one talks about baseball in Southern Nevada.

Jim Gemma remembers UNLV coach Fred Dallimore as the person that put UNLV baseball on the map. "He did everything to build baseball, to create a strong tradition, he recruited good players and he did many fundraisers. He was loyal and would do anything for you. During the time he made rebel baseball like a family. He was like a second father to me." Gemma said.

Shawn Barton

Shawn Barton was the pitching coach for the Las Vegas 51s, the AAA affiliate of the Los Angeles Dodgers (2002-2003). Barton is coaching in his third season (2003) with the Dodger organization and his second at the AAA level in Las Vegas. Barton also played major league baseball for three seasons with the San Francisco Giants and the Seattle Mariners. Barton pitched for the University of Nevada in 1984, pitching 119 innings with 87 strikeouts and seven complete games.

Shawn Barton was very interesting to talk with, maybe the reason for that was that we shared an Alma Mater in the University of Nevada. Maybe the reason was that we both are big fans of baseball and enjoy all aspects of the game. I'm not sure the reason I had the connection, whatever it was, I had a good time interviewing Shawn.

I started off asking him to compare his two years at Las Vegas. He described the 2002 squad the following way, "Power hitting was a key; we led the Pacific Coast League in wins and it was difficult for me to get used to the movement of players between different levels. The team really just found ways to win." I think Shawn really knows the game. I watched him layout his towel on the dugout wall, his water and notebook. I could tell that he set everything out the same way for each game.

"This year's team is pitching very well. We are getting timely hitting, have team speed and have good defense. This team has good team chemistry and has the expectation to win. We don't make a lot of mental mistakes," Shawn said with pride.

I asked Shawn about Las Vegas 51s President and General Manager Don Logan, "He has done a lot for the team. He is a great baseball man; he meets our needs and is a class act."

Shawn had the opportunity to pitch against and to observe the future Hall of Famer Greg Maddux, and had a lot of fun doing so. "Maddux was a master of pitching; he was very well prepared and had good execution," according to Shawn.

I wanted to talk about the time that Shawn spent at the University of Nevada. He only spent one season there in 1984, but was teammates with Rob Richie, Jim Puzey, Ted Higgins and Larry Beinfest. Shawn had the following memories of the University of Nevada, "It's a great school and I made lots of friends there." Shawn got drafted in the 21st round of the draft and signed on the hood of a car for an $8,000 signing bonus. He was assigned to Bend, Oregon.

Russ Langer

Russ Langer is the voice of the Las Vegas 51s. He has been broadcasting 51s games since their inaugural season of 2000. Prior to arriving in Las Vegas, Russ broadcasted for the Albuquerque Dukes, Phoenix Firebirds, Springfield Cardinals, and Vero Beach Dodgers.

I was amazed at the amount of enthusiasm that Russ had. He has over 12 years of experience broadcasting professional baseball. He had some favorite memories. "I had the thrill to speak with one of the greatest sportscasters of all-time, Vin Scully. On another occasion, I was able to talk with Kevin Brown on a pitching day. That was a very rare opportunity. Tommy Lasorda was a wealth of knowledge, very corporative, fun and possessed a treasure chest of stories," Langer told me with a smile.

Russ has had the opportunity to be mentored by Paul Olden, now with KNX 1070 News Radio. Olden had previously broadcasted for the Tampa Bay Devil Rays, New York Yankees, California Angels and Cleveland Indians. Russ also worked with Ken Korach who is working with the Oakland Athletics, and Jerry Reuss of the Los Angeles Dodgers. This is an all-star collection of sportscasters and I see no reason why Russ will not be joining them soon as a major league announcer.

I feel fortunate to have had the opportunity to talk with Russ and feel that he has a very bright future. In addition, Russ Langer has a goal, "I have the goal of getting to the majors. I would enjoy working in a good city." Good luck Russ!!

Russ met and worked briefly with former Las Vegas 51s Manager John Shoemaker in 1988 at Vero Beach, Florida the former spring training site of the Dodgers. It took some 14 seasons until the two would work together again.

John Shoemaker

John Shoemaker was the manager of the Las Vegas 51s for the 2003 season. He has been a member of the Dodger organization since 1977 serving as a player, coach, manager and instructor. Mr. Shoemaker has another interesting tie to Nevada as he played at Reno's Moana stadium while playing for the Lodi Dodgers in 1978.

I decided to talk with Mr. Shoemaker about his time spent in Reno. He had the following memories of Moana Stadium, "There was lots of wind and the lighting was poor. The bases were under water once when we were there." Mr. Shoemaker played with Ron Roenick, Max Venable, and Mark Bradley with Lodi. Eddie Watt was the manager at Reno.

The best memory that Mr. Shoemaker had was when he watched Al Campanis, who at the time was the General Manager of the Los Angeles Dodgers, "I watched Al Campanis show 2nd basemen how to field in Reno," Shoemaker told me with a smile.

It seemed to me that Shoemaker has enjoyed his time in baseball. He is a strong leader, and at the same time, a quiet leader. He is a student of the game and watches the subtle as well as the major aspects of the game. He was willing even though he had never met me, to allow me to have access to the dugout until just before the game. I was allowed to interview the pitching coach Shawn Barton in the dugout as well. It was the most time that I had spent in the dugout for years, and I feel fortunate to have had the opportunity to do this in 2003.

Ken Korach

Ken Korach is the current play-by-play radio announcer for the Oakland Athletics. He was the full time Las Vegas Stars radio announcer from 1989 to 1991 and split his time between the Chicago White Sox and Stars from 1992 to 1995.

Korach has some great memories about baseball in Las Vegas, "Cashman Field is the most beautiful park in the Pacific Coast League. Las Vegas is the best place for AAA baseball. There is a lot of energy with the crowd. The Stars are a model franchise; they are run very well. There is a big-time feel with baseball in Las Vegas. Big League Weekend is an incredible event. In 1993, Harry Caray (the long-time Chicago Cubs announcer) was there, it was an amazing feel for a spring training game. Big League Weekend gives the City of Las Vegas exposure and that is good for the city."

When the 1996 baseball season opened it was bittersweet for Ken Korach. The Oakland A's had to open the season on the road in Las Vegas and Ken was working for the White Sox. "I was the story. I was from Las Vegas and now I was back in Las Vegas. It was strange," Korach remembered.

Korach enjoys a very strong relationship with Don Logan, the President and General Manager of the Las Vegas Stars. "Logan does a first class job in Las Vegas. He is a special person in my life he has done a lot for me in my professional life. He is very well respected. He is Mr. Las Vegas. He is well connected in the baseball community. Don has a very good feel for baseball. He has always been supportive of me and my wife (Denise currently works for the 51s), allowing me to schedule my work week on my own. He is a good reference. We even play golf together."

The former owner of the Las Vegas Stars was Larry Koentopp who moved the team from Spokane, Washington to Las Vegas in 1983. Ken Korach remembers Koentopp "as a very good owner I have a lot of respect for him."

Sandy Alomar Jr. was the best player that Korach remembers playing in Las Vegas. "He handled everything graciously he was a very remarkable player."

Ken Korach continues to make Las Vegas his off-season home.

Bruce Bochy

Bruce Bochy is the current skipper of the National League's San Francisco Giants played and coached baseball in Nevada. When, you ask? He played for the Las Vegas Stars in 1983, 1984 and 1988 and managed in the California League in 1990 and 1991 making stops at Reno's historic Moana Stadium (where I first met him). I had the opportunity to interview him before an interleague game in Oakland, California on June 7, 2000.

"Bochy" has some great memories of playing in Las Vegas, "I had never been to Vegas before. There was a playoff atmosphere before the first game (played at Cashman Field). There was an enthusiasm and energy that I had never experienced before. There was great fan support and excitement during the first year. It (playing) was an experience I'll never forget."

Bruce Bochy #15 Playing for the Las Vegas Stars
Courtesy: Las Vegas 51s

Bochy hit the first home run in Las Vegas Stars history. He played with Kevin McReynolds and Tim Flannery. All three made it to the Majors. Bochy first met Kevin McReynolds in Las Vegas, "He (McReynolds) had a great talent to hit the baseball and he was very unassuming," Bochy recalled. Tim Flannery has been Bochy's third base coach since the 1996 baseball season.

UNLV

Bill Ireland

The late Bill Ireland, nicknamed "Coach I," grew up in McGill, Nevada and graduated from the University of Nevada in 1952. He played and coached for Jack Threlkel's Reno Garage teams. He coached baseball at Fernley High School, South Tahoe High School and at the University of Nevada from 1960 to 1967. During his tenure at Nevada he never had a losing season. The University of Nevada won the Pacific Division Championship in 1965 and was runner-up in 1966. Ireland had the opportunity to coach the most successful collegiate coaches in Nevada, Fred Dallimore (UNLV) and Gary Powers (Nevada), both as players. Mr. Ireland was the first football coach at Nevada Southern University (now UNLV). He was promoted to the position of UNLV athletic director in 1973 and served in that capacity until 1980.

Ireland remembers that the state of Nevada was a lot different in the 1940's and 1950's, "Everybody knew everybody. There was one university in Nevada and that was in Reno, everybody went to Reno." Ireland met his wife Jean at the University of Nevada. Bill and Jean Ireland lived in the married housing units then called *Victory Heights*. This is where they met their lifelong friends Rollan and Marilyn Melton who were their next-door neighbors. "Bill and I would carry on through-the-wall conversations as we both would use the bathroom at the same time[5]", Melton writes. "Rollan was a great sportswriter and friend," Ireland stated.

The University of Nevada was also very different. The baseball team practiced and played some games at Clark Field (which is now the site of the Education Building.) The team played the majority of their baseball games in Reno's Moana Stadium. During

---

[5] Page 69, Sonny's Story: A Journalists Memoir, Rollan Melton, University of Nevada Reno Oral History Program, 1999.

this time there was not any politics and the team was welcome to play at Moana. If there was a conflict the team would simply play at Clark Field.

Nevada made a really exciting road trip to play against Nevada Southern Bill Ireland's team in Las Vegas:

> "On the way to Las Vegas to play a game at Nevada Southern (UNLV) the Nevada team stopped and had lunch at the Mizpah Hotel in Tonopah. Shortly after the team left, their luggage fell off the van and Lorne Wagner lost everything but his pants. The team continued on to Las Vegas and plays their game at the Old Cashman field. Nevada won the game. The team started back to Reno and again stopped at Tonopah. When the team went into the Mizpah, they saw that somebody was wearing Wagner's jersey. The whole team started laughing."
>
> Former University of Nevada
> player Ron Pagni

The team traveled in a white van called the "Gray Whale" it seated 12 and luggage was strapped to the top.

The team also played a few very interesting games in Northern Nevada. The University of Notre Dame played a game against the University of Nevada in Fallon. The game was played in Fallon because they paid the guarantee, meaning that there was an amount of money that was guaranteed to the team no matter if they won or lost. Notre Dame got the gate receipts, but Nevada won the game 16-15, the game started on a Thursday and ended after midnight on Good Friday. Nevada also played a game against USC; this game was played in Reno and USC won the game 7 to 4.

Some of the players that Ireland coached at Nevada were Nik Walters, Ron Pagni, Don "Bo Bolinsky" Weir, Gordon "Gordy" Lemich, Lorne "Daddy Wags" Wagner, Gary Powers, Fred Dallimore and Bruce Nickerson. Many of these players would play for the Fallon Merchants of the Sierra Nevada League during the summer months. The Fallon Merchants were owned by Marty Townsend. I will state again that the greatest professional compliment anyone can have is to be complemented with a kind word from a professional peer. A few former players gave me quotes about Bill Ireland:

- "Ireland was personable. He cared for you. He kept us in line. He was motivational and was fun to be around," Ron Pagni.
- He (Ireland) was great to play for. I would not want to play for anyone else," Nik Walters.

The image that I came away with from the interview was the infectious smile of Bill Ireland. He was a very smart man, always thinking. I got the feeling that he was very happy and content with his life.

Mr. Ireland had a tremendous impact on the future of college baseball in Nevada as he coached the next two University of Nevada coaches. I feel very fortunate that I was able to meet and talk with Mr. Ireland and am thankful for his openness in regards to his part of Nevada Baseball history.

Fred Dallimore

During his high school playing days, Fred Dallimore was coached by the late Reno High School legend Dr. Bud Beasley. "I love Bud. I learned about (baseball) techniques and philosophy. Bud communicated in a funny way. He took a personal interest in my development. Bud always said; never let your size determine how you play the game. Bud was tenacious. One of things I admire most about him is he is happy and content with life. I am very glad that he was part of my life. I have lots of respect for him and we had lots of fun as well."

In 1962, Dallimore won his first meaningful championship, the High School Championship.

Prior to becoming the head coach at UNLV, Dallimore served as an assistant under Coach Bob Doering from 1969 to 1973. Dallimore played baseball at the University of Nevada, Reno from 1963 to 1966. The 1963 Nevada baseball team was coached by Dallimore's life-long friend and mentor Bill Ireland. Dallimore has a huge amount of respect for Ireland. "He was really a second father to me, one of the only guys to take an interest in my development. He recruited me. We had lots in common: mining backgrounds, Native

Nevadans. He liked what I stood for. Our relationship grew and grew. (Ireland) took me to Las Vegas as a kid. Bill knew education was important to (my) Dad," Dallimore recalled with fond emotion. This was a great story behind the story and once again, I felt very fortunate to have heard it.

While a player at the University of Nevada, Reno, Fred Dallimore played for legendary coach Jackie Jensen (the 1958 American League MVP). Dallimore remembers Jensen as "a great athlete. He also had a good base of knowledge about baseball."

Between the 1965 and 1966 seasons, Dallimore played on the semi-pro Fallon Merchant squad. The team played in the very competitive Sierra Nevada League. The team played at the National Baseball Congress tournament in Liberal, Kansas in 1966.

I had the opportunity to interview former UNLV head baseball coach Fred Dallimore. He summarized his coaching philosophy in this quote, "You can do anything if you execute your plan." He also believes that any plan is better than no plan and that there is no substitution for hard work. Dallimore possesses a tenacious work ethic; "No one will ever out work me," Dallimore stated. He acquired his strong work ethic from his dad, Johnny.

During his 23 years (1974 to 1996) as the UNLV head baseball coach, Fred Dallimore was very dedicated to the University. He compiled a coaching record of 794 wins and 558 losses. UNLV appeared in seven NCAA Regional Tournaments under coach Dallimore and had their best year in 1980.

1980 UNLV Team Summary
- Won 53 games, lost 13, 1 tie
- Ranked as high as #4 in the National Polls
- Made it within one game of reaching the College World Series

Coach Dallimore had a great relationship with former Carson High School Coach Ron McNutt. Every year Coach Dallimore would travel to Northern Nevada to recruit players to play at UNLV. He used his roots to take players to the South. The way that Coach Dallimore figured it, "If they were good (players) in the short season (of Northern Nevada), I could turn them into blue chip baseball players in the South."

The most famous baseball player that Dallimore coached was former major league third baseman Matt Williams. Dallimore remembers the following about Matt Williams, "He knew what he wanted in life. He wanted to play in the Majors. He was very demanding on physical strength (batting), he did everything he could to become the best baseball player. (He possesses the) same values now as he has always had. Matt is a great competitor a good person and he gives back to the community. Williams comes from a good family."

While Matt Williams played at UNLV, Coach Dallimore moved him from 3rd base to shortstop to utilize the quick feet of Williams.

Matt Williams (Courtesy Arizona Diamondbacks)

Once again, I think some of the highest praise comes when others in your professional field complement you. While attending the 2000 Stanford Regional, I asked two opposing coaches about Coach Dallimore. Stanford head baseball coach Mark Marquess had praise for Dallimore, "He established a program and was well respected. He was fiery and was always well prepared. I was sorry to see him go." Fresno State head baseball coach Bob Bennett said, "Dallimore was one-of-a-kind. He was a dear friend...we are real good friends. He was a good coach. Dallimore did a lot that went unnoticed. There is no better competitor than Fred."

Coach Dallimore also had a good relationship with Rodger Fairless, the legendary high school coach from Las Vegas. "He was a good player and he made himself the coach that he is today, through attending clinics. He was demanding and a well disciplined coach," Dallimore praised.

UNLV players that played for Dallimore who went on to the Majors

1.) Matt Williams	11.) Tommy Tellman
2.) Scott Lewis	12.) Vance McHenry
3.) Donovan Osborne	13.) Eric Ludwick
4.) Todd Stottlemyre	14.) Bill Scherrer
5.) T.J. Matthews	15.) Bob Aryault
6.) Brian Boehringer	16.) Ralph Garcia
7.) Cecil Fielder	
8.) Bip Roberts	
9.) Marty Cordova	
10.) Joe Bover	

UNLV Coaching Records

Name	Years	Win	Loss	Tie	%
"Chub" Drakulich	1960-1966	*			
Bob Doering	1967-1973	158	127	3	.554
Fred Dallimore	1974-1996	794	558	2	.587
Rod Soesbe	1997-2001	129	155		.454
Jim Schlossnagle	2002-2003	77	47		.621
Buddy Gouldsmith	2004-	147	156		.485

* records were not kept until 1967

UNLV Players

Brian Boehringer played at the University of Nevada Las Vegas in 1990 and 1991 and was drafted in 1990 by the Houston Astros in the 10th round. Boehringer was a right-handed pitcher that played on the NY Yankees, San Diego Padres, San Francisco Giants and Pittsburgh Pirates. He was on the 1996 Yankees squad that won the World Series as well as on the Padre team that won the National League Pennant in 1998. When I interviewed Brian he was playing in Oakland on the San Diego Padres in 2000 for an interleague game after talking with him I went over to the A's clubhouse and talked with his former teammate T.J. Mathews went to the same junior college, Meremac Junior College in St. Louis, Missouri and UNLV and ultimately to the Majors.

Boehringer got along well with former UNLV Coach Dallimore. "He was a good conditioning coach, he provided good assistance and I enjoyed playing college ball at UNLV," Boehringer reminisced. Boehringer was also teammates with another future major leaguer Donovan Osborne.

T.J. Mathews pitched for eight Major League seasons and he played his college baseball at UNLV. T.J talked with admiration of UNLV, "I have great memories of playing baseball at UNLV. I loved it there. Coach Dallimore was the most interesting person that I have ever met. He is a great pitching coach. I would not trade it (UNLV career) for anything. There are lots of good people at UNLV. It was too bad that we had to play at the old stadium (Rebel Field)." Art Howe, while manager of the Oakland Athletics, said, "T.J. is a big part of our bull pen. We depend on him a lot."

Travis McClendon played on the UNLV team from 1994-1995. Travis knew what Coach Dallimore expected from him and that he was able to do it. He most memorable collegiate games were against Reno. "The games were intense; Peccole Park was full. One year Chris Briones hit the game winning home run off us. It was an awesome game!" McClendon remembered.

Matt Williams played high school baseball at Carson High under coach Ron McNutt and at UNLV under former head coach Fred Dallimore. Williams is the only baseball player in the history of UNLV baseball to have his uniform number retired. His #15 was retired before a UNLV basketball game on December 22, 1990.

I had the great opportunity to talk with my favorite baseball player about Matt Williams and this is what Tony Gwynn told me, "He is really a good player. He came up as a shortstop and made himself into a top hitter. He has been solid from the beginning."

Former Major League Manager Buck Showalter said, "We are lucky to have him around. He leads by example. He is a special breed of ballplayer, one that I hope does not die. He holds himself to a high standard. There is not a more respected player in baseball than Matt Williams." Former All-Star Diamondbacks outfielder Luis Gonzalez said, "Matt is a great competitor. He is intense; a great teammate and a great dad. He is always playing with his kid. He is fun to watch."

"I'm proud of Matt, as he has accomplished what he has set out to do (in life)...that is to play baseball. He always knew what he wanted to do with his talent and that was to play professional baseball. Baseball is the only thing that Matt has ever wanted to do." Arthur Williams (Matt's dad) recalled about his son.

9th Inning: The Future

As I contemplate the future of professional baseball in Reno with the arrival of the Reno Aces (AAA affiliate of the Arizona Diamondbacks) in 2009, I must take a step back before moving into the future. It has often been written that you cannot move into the future without taking a quick glimpse into the past.

I need to talk a little about the demise of Moana Stadium. I watched games there and saw that work needed to be done. In fact, Minor League baseball even came up with deficiencies that were defined and they mailed this list to the management of the Reno professional ball clubs. Some of these requirements were fixed such as stadium lighting, stadium seating (with seatbacks), and infield and outfield playing surface enhancements. Some of them, however, were not fixed, including increased restroom facilities, increased stadium seating capacity and improved locker room facilities. The last time that a professional baseball game was played at Moana was 17 seasons ago. Wow! That makes me feel old.

One thing led to another and soon—all too soon for me—the teams left. I say this was too soon because I was just starting to learn about the game. To their credit, several ownership groups came in and tried to revive the team. These teams were known as the Reno Chukkars and the Reno Blackjacks but, it just was not the same. I even worked for one summer with the Chuckars and had fun, but it did not compare to having real major league prospects come into your town. When you have this affiliation you have prospects and teams that have ties to the majors. You know what you are going to get. It is a real tangible thing.

Over the next 15 years there were many rumors about teams coming in. Some wanted to fix Moana Stadium up, some wanted to build a new ballpark. But it was all just that talk, nothing more. As a fan, it was frustrating not having professional baseball.

The City of Sparks tried with valiant effort to create an entertainment district at the Sparks Marina. They had many, many discussions with an organization called Sierra Nevada baseball. There was excitement for the first time in many, many years. They even had a website and things were moving along very well. However, the champion of Sierra Nevada baseball, CJ Jones, died before this vision could be realized. Sparks was still working to secure a stadium and a team but…could not get the deal done.

City of Reno officials had different ideas and they came in during the 9th inning and jumped in and got things done very quickly. It all happened just a few days prior to the sun setting of funds allotted by the 2005 Legislature (these funds were part of the new rental car tax), the City was able to get a deal done and hit the ball out of the park. Soon it was announced that there would be a new stadium constructed at the intersection of 2nd Street and Evans just east of the Reno Bowling Stadium.

Ground was broken in February 2008 and the development of the site was underway. I wanted to be at the groundbreaking ceremony but had prior commitments and was not able to attend. What was amazing to me is that people that I talked with recently were skeptical that a team was coming. There was still an air of disbelief that Reno could actually be getting a professional baseball team.

I, however, was not one of the doubters. I visited the construction site on several occasions and watched its progress. In fact, I have taken the following photos to show its progress. For me, there is fun in watching construction. It takes me back to my youth. I watched the construction of US 395 from Oddie Boulevard south. I witnessed the building of the MGM Grand, the Atlantis, and numerous other casino expansions. There is just something about steel and concrete. The following photos show the construction of the stadium.

Reno Aces Ballpark Photos

Aces Ballpark Construction September 2008 (Tim Mueller)

Aces Ballpark Construction March 2009 (Courtesy Reno Aces)

(used with permission)

When I attended to the "Name the Team" celebration at the Sierra Hotel and Spa on September 23, 2008, I felt proud almost like a proud papa after the birth of a child. The team actually had arrived! What made the time that much more special was I was one of the 58 people who had submitted the name "Reno Aces" for the new team. I was excited and felt a real connection to the team. I wondered about many things...What the uniform would look like? What it would be like to watch a game at the new stadium? What the mascot will look like? Which baseball players will I be able to follow when they play for the Aces and even the opponents of the Aces? I will likely do the same types of things that I did prior to 1992 like notate broken bats and asking for autographs. 16 years is a long time. What has changed? What is the same about this game that I am such a fan of? I might even go off the deep end and start my own database of players and teams seen charting my own stats. Things like the oldest and the youngest players to play for and against the Aces, the first walk, the first hit batter, the most famous player, the top prospect. You never know as I have been a member of the Society of American Baseball Research (SABR) since 1998.

I have made the trek, albeit it not a far one to Reno, to watch the progress of the stadium construction. I enjoy seeing construction activity especially when it has been something that many, many people have been hoping for a long time and to see it become a reality is very special. I looked through some old files and found a story talking about the possibility of building a new stadium in 1997. Talk resurfaced again in 2004 but it took until 2007 to get the project off the ground.

The Reno-Tahoe region will share an identity of being listed with other teams that on the AAA list places like Las Vegas, Sacramento, Salt Lake City, Colorado Springs, Portland, Tacoma, Fresno, Omaha, New Orleans, Nashville, Memphis and Albuquerque. That is some great exposure and when it is seen and mentioned over and over again in newspapers, websites and cable sports networks it is almost like a marketing plan of its own. It puts you on the map in a way that only sports, especially baseball, can.

It is an exciting time for me, local baseball fans, the City of Reno, Northern Nevada and for the State of Nevada. Baseball has returned to the area and it seems like it will be there for a long time.

Reno Aces History

City/team	Years
San Francisco Seals	1903-1957
Phoenix Giants	1958-1959
Tacoma Giants	1960-1965
Phoenix Giants/Firebirds	1966-1996
Tucson Toros/Sidewinders	1997-2008
Reno Aces	2009 to ???

When I look at the above list I think about the names of Joe DiMaggio and Lefty O'Doul of the San Francisco Seals. I even think about Ted Williams playing on the opposing San Diego Padres (then a PCL team). I think of games at a stadium that I never had the privilege of visiting—San Francisco's Seals Stadium. I think of the price of tickets and how much hot dogs were in the old days. I think of old cars and formal dress. I think of World War I and World War II. The team survived and I know that it enjoyed many wonderful seasons. I don't think Reno will have any trouble duplicating that.

It also intrigues me that former University of Nevada baseball star Lyle Overbay could have played for the hometown Aces if the team had moved to Reno ten years earlier.

(used with permission)

The Las Vegas franchise has provided an excellent source of family entertainment for a quarter century. The team has hosted "Big League Weekend", AAA All Star game and a League Championship. The team won the Pacific Coast League Championship in 1986 and 1988.

This history of the Las Vegas 51s is more current. They have called the Silver State their home since 1983. They began playing at Cashman Field on April 10, 1983 a date that they also won their first game by a score of 11-8 over the visiting Salt Lake

Las Vegas 51s History

Team Name	Affiliation	Years
Las Vegas Stars	Padres	1983-2000
Las Vegas 51s	Dodgers	2001-2008
Las Vegas 51s	Blue Jays	2009-???

I can only imagine a new Nevada sports rivalry starting each year the Reno Aces and Las Vegas 51s will play 16 games against each other as they will be competing in the Pacific Coast League's Pacific South division. 16 games could be the difference between first and third places. I know from attending many UNR and UNLV games through the years that this will be a fun 'intense' rivalry. I don't think it will take long to start up either my guess is by the time the second or third series are being played that they players and coaches will have plenty of motivation.

I am personally looking forward to seeing major league prospects or injured major leaguers on rehab assignments play in Reno. I am also interested to see how the new stadium looks, what food is available and what views are afforded.

The team also came up with a marketing plan in which they would market the team in part with a simple slogan "Aceball is here!" This would be a way to connect the team name with the sport it plays. It is a catchy yet brief slogan; one that I think is already successful. I have been impressed with the front office staff of the Aces in their talents and professionalism.

I attended the "Meet the Manager" Dinner on January 21, 2009 at the Reno Ballroom. It was my first time inside this great meeting venue. I considered this dinner a great opportunity to interact with the Aces front office staff and to meet their first season manager Brett Butler. It was surreal to meet Brett as I had been a "closet fan" of his (as a Padre fan, I could not root for the Giants or Dodgers). I enjoyed his work ethic and his thirst of the game. He always ran out every ball that he hit. He was not afraid to get his uniform dirty and he was a quiet leader who led by example. I want my life to follow his in terms of his leadership and faith. He was a great speaker who was able to weave his personal life and baseball life together. He talked about his cancer and his fight to overcome it. It was very inspirational in both words and actions. I had a great time.

I also had scheduled a meeting with Branch Rickey III, the grandson of Branch Rickey Sr., who broke baseball's color barrier by signing Jackie Robinson to play major league baseball for the Brooklyn Dodgers in 1947. I was able to meet with Mr. Rickey and we talked about my project. It was a great time of interaction and a ton of fun to connect with a person who dripped baseball history. He was very conversational and it was like talking with a good friend after church, very comfortable. He and I talked about the upcoming season of "Aceball" and he even had the suggestion that I end this book with this chapter.

As Branch spoke at the dinner, he talked about the reality of the Aces starting play and he got the crowd to repeat, "The Aces are coming, the Aces are coming, the Aces are coming." To hear the crowd of some 400 chant "The Aces are coming," on a January night was awesome. I wondered what the stadium would look like, how it would feel, who would get the first hit, who would throw the first pitch. There are many unknowns.

What is known is that the team will be playing in a state-of-the-art stadium at the intersection of 2nd and Evans streets in downtown Reno. It will have many amenities that are just dreams to countless minor league stadiums. It will be part of a larger entertainment district that will eventually include restaurants and shops. It will be a destination location. One could come to a game and relax watching a game at a tremendous baseball venue then stroll through shops and enjoy a nice meal. What could be better? This scene is exciting to me and one that I am looking forward to.

Now imagine with me for a moment: it is the first game of the season, the stadium is packed with fans and the announcer starts calling out the names of the Reno Aces. "Now playing first base is…at second is…" the players run out to their positions and they take infield practice. The infield dirt is marked for the first time. The crowd goes wild and they are anticipating who will win this game. Some may think back to games they have attended in a previous season either in Reno or elsewhere. Baseball fans are sentimental folks that enjoy the historical ties and memories of the past.

I will be thinking back to my time spent at a ballpark not too far away from this one at least in terms of geography, but a ballpark thousands of miles away in terms of architecture, fan experience and modern conveniences. This ballpark where the Aces will play will be a treat, a diamond in the rough, someplace to bring out-of-town visitors, a place to be proud of.

Soon…the umpire yells, "Play Ball" the season is underway, the wait is over, and baseball is back in Reno—this time for a very long time. "Aceball" is here to stay. Are you game? I am!!

Extra Innings: Player Snippets

The goal of this section is to include player interviews that did not fit into other portions of the book. That is not to say that they are not important. In fact, the first snippet of Dean Bonfigli is very important to me personally. I did not want to leave this out as there is some very interesting information. Enjoy!!

Dean Bonfigli played 2nd base for the Nevada Wolf Pack from 1990 to 1993. His baseball career coincided with my academic stint at the University of Nevada. We had a class together and developed a good relationship over the course of the school year. I learned about what it was like to play baseball at the collegiate level. I was amazed by the amount of practice and the travel demands of being a college baseball player. At times I felt like I was on the team from the aspect of knowing what was happening with the team from a mental aspect.

Vince Coleman former Major League Player had some ties to Nevada players he played against both Greg Maddux and Matt Williams. "Greg Maddux is one of the most dominant pitchers in the National League. He is intelligent; he finesses you and does not beat himself," Colman said. Coleman also played against former Arizona Diamondbacks player Matt Williams who played his high school baseball in Carson City and his collegiate baseball at UNLV. Coleman said of Williams, "He is a great defensive third-baseman; he fit in well with the Giants 'Murders Row.'" (Will Clark, Kevin Mitchell and Williams).

Coleman often faced Bobby Cox's Atlanta Braves and thought he would have enjoyed the opportunity to play for Cox. "He is an old-school manager similar to Whitey Herzog and Chuck Tanner; (he's) a players' manager, and he allows you to steal bases," Colman reminisced at the Celebrity Golf Tournament at Edgewood Tahoe. I enjoyed just watching Vince Coleman's eyes sparkle when he thought of what may have been if he ever had the opportunity to wear a Braves uniform.

Nick Day graduated from Green Valley High School (Las Vegas) in 1996, after leading Green Valley to 4 State Championships, was awarded the 1996 Gatorade Nevada High School Player of the Year after hitting .482. He was drafted in the 15th round of the 1996 Draft by the Pittsburgh Pirates. He signed a letter of intent to play at Stanford University and played there from 1997 to 1999.

Day remembered his high school days as, "Intense. We were practicing every day. We worked harder than anyone and it was very competitive. Everyone (players and coaches) expected us to win the State Championship every year." Coach Fairless remembers Nick Day as an "excellent athlete possessing good size and speed, a hard worker, a great kid both on and off the field and having a great arm along with having a very competitive attitude."

Mike Dotterer played baseball at Reno High School (1976-1977) and on the Reno Babe Ruth team. Dotterer then transferred to Edison (CA) High School to play his junior and senior seasons. Mike then played in a high school baseball tournament with both Bobby Mecham and Tony Gwynn.

Mike continued to play baseball at Stanford University and played both football and baseball with John Elway in 1980. Mike said, "John Elway was a hard thrower."

According to John Elway, "Mike was a great athlete he could do it all. He was a great bunter, energetic, unique and a character." It was a lot of fun talking with a future football Hall of Famer about his days before he threw the pigskin. I got the feeling that John Elway really enjoyed having Mike Dotterer as a teammate. Mike also played on the 1981 USA Baseball Team with Spike Owen.

"Dutch" Dotterer Mike's dad was one of only a few Major Leaguers to hit a grand slam off Sandy Koufax. "Dutch" played for 11 seasons 1951 to 1952 for the Cincinnati Reds. "Dutch" also made the highest catch at Cincinnati's Crosley Field.

Justin Drizos played college baseball at the University of Nevada from 1994 to 1995. He played on the 1999 Reno Blackjacks team. Justin explained the difference between college and pro baseball

114

in this way, "There is more time to make adjustments to your game in college. In order to make it to the Major Leagues, it takes a lot of hard work."

Justin has some great memories of playing baseball at the University of Nevada. "In my junior year 1994 when we won the Big West conference, it was a special year, with some great teammates; we got a ring and memories that will never go away."

Rollie Fingers The Hall of Fame pitcher played for the Oakland A's, San Diego Padres and Milwaukee. Fingers has a Nevada connection as well. He played for Dick Williams in Oakland and post-baseball, both now live in Las Vegas. According to Rollie Fingers "Dick Williams managed a pitching staff better than anyone else that I knew. He did not like mental errors."

Chris Kahl played at the University of Nevada from 1996 to 1998. He also played on the semi-pro Reno Blackjacks in 1999. Kahl enjoyed both teams at the college level; the focus of the team was on teamwork. At the professional level, it focused more on individual development. Kahl remembers Coach Powers as wanting to get the most out of his players. I respect what Coach Powers does, both on and off the field. Former Carson High star Charley Kerfeld was the Blackjacks coach in 1999, and Kahl described him this way, "He has great passion for the game; he is a good teacher and he loves to win." Kahl had his best baseball memories as having the chance to play pro baseball with the Blackjacks and getting his first college hit against Fresno State. Chris would like to coach one day.

Justin Martin played at the University of Nevada from 1996 to 1999. He was then drafted by the Pittsburgh Pirates in the 1999 Amateur Baseball Draft. After our interview on February 29, 2000, just before Martin left for spring training, I felt like we began a friendship.

We talked about his reflections playing for the Nevada Wolf Pack. We talked about snow falling on the field and shoveling snow off the field. Nevada enjoys a home field advantage that is not shared by many other schools, "Home field advantage (at Nevada) means 32 degrees and snow. One year, Long Beach State left sunshine and 98 degrees, came to Reno and played in snow. Stanford even shoveled snow here." Martin always enjoyed the annual Bobby Dolan Baseball dinner. "I enjoyed the fans and the video highlights. The Nevada fans are dedicated, they want to know the players and they take a real interest in the players. It's kind of like they own stock and they want to see how their investment is doing. They talk with you at the malls and are really nice people and they want you to succeed."

Matt Ortiz played on the University of Nevada baseball teams from 1998 to 2000 seasons. Ortiz had the opportunity to play for Loyola Maramount, University of Miami, San Diego State and the University of San Francisco. But chose to play at the University of Nevada for a few reasons, "I was recruited by (then Nevada Assistant Coach) John Savage. Nevada was a choice program, a program on the rise. I wanted to be part of a great program. Coach Powers is an excellent coach. I was excited to be playing for the University of Nevada", Ortiz said.

Matt Ortiz played with Lyle Overbay on the 1999 Nevada squad. He paid Overbay the following complements, "He can do nothing and make the team better just through his presence in the lineup. Something big could happen at any moment because he is that good of a hitter. The other team is going to have to pitch around him because he puts up great numbers. He is a tremendous hitter; he is also a great clutch hitter. His presence in the lineup is enough. He can do nothing, and by just being in the lineup, changes the game."

Bob Peccole played for the Sierra Royals during the 1939 and 1940 seasons. His brother Bill was a good ballplayer as well. The Peccoles started American Legion baseball in Las Vegas. Peccole remembers Myron Levitt played American Legion baseball. Peccole remembers that life, in general, was much more difficult in those days, "I quit baseball to go to work, as things were tough in those days. You had to scratch for food, just to eat; however, baseball has done a lot for our family, politically, and in every shape and form. And that's what has made the family."

In addition, Peccole tried his hand at owning a ball club. He set up a meeting with Jack Threlkel in 1942, and asked him if he would be willing to sell the Reno Garage club. He said he might if the price was right. "Tell me what you have in mind," Threlkel said. "We exchanged amounts on pieces of paper, finally after much negotiation, he agreed to sell the club to De Lorenzi and me," Peccole said proudly.

Daryl Reynolds played for St. Mary's College Red Sox (CA) baseball team before playing on the Lovelock Nevada baseball team from 1939 to 1941. Lovelock played in the very competitive Sierra Nevada League. Bill Milich owned the Lovelock club. Mr. Reynolds had a really good quote that really showed what the game was like in the past, "We had more fun in 2 minutes than the new modern players do in a season."

Along with being a very good baseball player, Mr. Reynolds also helped to start the Reno area Little League program with Jack Teague.

Mr. Reynolds tells an interesting story from his childhood. In 1935, he had gone to Bay Meadows Race Track in San Mateo with some friends. While using the restroom he looked down on the floor and saw a "big gold ring". "I picked it up and it had the initials L.O.D. engraved on it. It was the 1934 World Series Championship ring and it belonged to Lefty O' Doul. I told an usher about it and he notified O'Doul. Lefty came by the Village Café on Lombard Street in San Francisco and picked up the ring and left me a $20 check, which was quite a reward in those days," Reynolds beamed, as he recalled this wonderful piece of baseball history.

Chris Singleton played at the University of Nevada from 1993 to 1994 before being drafted by the San Francisco Giants in the 2nd round of the 1993 Amateur Baseball Draft. He played for six Major League seasons with the Chicago White Sox, Baltimore Orioles, Oakland A's and Tampa Bay Rays. Former Major League Manager, Buck Showalter, said, "(Singleton) is a very gifted athlete. He has worked hard, and is now getting the opportunity to play."

Charley Smith played on the Los Angeles Dodgers, Philadelphia Phillies, Chicago White Sox, New York Mets, St. Louis Cardinals, New York Yankees and Chicago Cubs from 1960 to 1969. His connection with Northern Nevada was largely due to the meeting of his soon to be wife, the former Carol Richards of Sparks, Nevada.

Charley enjoyed the outdoor activities of the region including hunting and fishing. His love of the outdoors added to his "new love" and Northern Nevada became home.

Carol Smith widow of Charley Smith did not consider herself a baseball fan prior to meeting Charley. She did enjoy watching Charley play. Carol stated, "I would rather read, paint or garden than watch sports." Carol admitted, "My sister was a bigger baseball fan than I was." One of Carol's favorite memories was when she appeared on the TV Password Quiz Show with some of the other Mets players' wives. She had a great time and enjoyed the friendships she developed.

Extra Innings: Coach Snippets

Coach Rodger Fairless coached baseball in the Las Vegas Valley first at El Dorado High School from 1978 to 1979, at Valley High School from 1980 to 1989, at UNLV in 1990 and at Green Valley High School from 1992 to 1998. He compiled a 493-80 win/loss record (.860%) in 19 seasons winning 12 State Championships. He was born in Las Vegas on November 28, 1951, graduated from Rancho High School and went to Southern Utah University.

He has been interested in baseball since he started playing the game at age seven. He played in both high school and college. He was both a pitcher and a first baseman.

Coach Fairless has a basic coaching philosophy of learning the fundamentals first, emphasizing hard work and discipline. Coach Fairless stated, "I have respect for former Carson High School baseball coach Ron McNutt, as he has produced some great ballplayers." He also enjoyed coaching at UNLV in 1990. Fairless continued, "I learned a lot from Coach Dallimore. He was fair with me."

Coach Fairless had a difficult time defining his favorite team. He said, "All the teams were different. The 1978 El Dorado team was special, as they had only 12 players and they didn't have a lot of overachievers. But all the teams shared one thing, and that was they all were unique in their own way."

A good ballplayer is separated from a great ballplayer according to Coach Fairless, "By their willingness to work hard and to listen. They have a (genuine) desire to do better."

Coach Fairless coached perennial All Star, Cy Young winner, and soon-to-be Hall of Famer, Greg Maddux. Coach has a special relationship with Mr. Maddux; they continue to talk and meet in the off season.

Coach Fairless has coached the following players who have played in the Majors:

Mike Morgan	Marty Barrett	Steve Chiltron
Greg Maddux	Doug Mirabelli	Tyler Houston
Mike Maddux	Chad Hermanson	Steve Rodriquez

Coach Ron McNutt coached at Carson High School from 1976 to2004 when he began coaching at Carson High, he was involved with the baseball, football and basketball programs. As the head baseball coach he compiled 655 wins against just 267 losses and won two State Championships. In addition, he would coach summer league baseball the team was called the Carson Capitols. He coached this team for 23 years leading them to an amazing 1,173 and 228 record. He was born in Ohio on July 17, 1943, graduated from Defiance High School (Ohio) and went to the College of Idaho.

He has been interested in baseball since he began collecting baseball cards as a kid. "It has always been something that I have enjoyed", McNutt said.

Coach McNutt had the following thoughts about coaching, "As long as I feel like I still have something to offer the kids and I enjoy myself, I still want to coach. I will know when the time is right (to retire). I have been coaching at Carson High School since 1976 and I really enjoy it. I am also to the point where I am looking forward to the end of my teaching career."

Coach McNutt is very proud of what he has accomplished since coming to Carson High School. The baseball program has received a lot of community support. The community has donated building materials, labor and money to benefit the baseball program. "The community has made (the program) what it is today," McNutt stated. McNutt is happy that he has chosen the career of a baseball coach. The community has made his job a lot easier. "I love Carson City," McNutt beams.

It was refreshing for me to learn that Coach McNutt made many career choices based on his priority of placing family first. He has given his family priority above baseball and I applaud him for that. Family is put before baseball in the McNutt household. Coach McNutt is a humble man. When he started coaching, he did not know he was going to be coach for 25 years. Coach McNutt admitted, "It just happened."

Another prominent Coach Rodger Fairless stated, "I have respect for Carson High School baseball coach Ron McNutt; he has produced some great ballplayers." Coach McNutt coached the following Major Leaguers; Charley Kerfeld, Matt Williams, Bob Ayrault and Donovan Osborne.

"Certain individuals have God-given talent; these kids all had something very special. They work very hard, but you could see the talent they had," Coach Ron McNutt said of Kerfeld, Williams Ayrault and Osborne.

Coach McNutt has coached the following players who have been drafted or who are playing in the Majors:

Mike Shoaf	Jim Good	Mike Pintar
Darryl Rasner	Charley Kerfeld	Matt Williams
Mike Dandos	Dusty Bergman	Bob Ayrault
Donovan Osborne	Sean Johnson	Scott Bibee
Dean Madsen	Nate Yeskie	David Lundquist

The most surprising part of the interview occurred when I asked Coach McNutt about the connection to the UNLV baseball program. There was a pipeline of baseball players to Southern Nevada, as McNutt's students Matt Williams, Donovan Osborne and Nate Yeskie went on to play under UNLV coach Fred Dallimore. "Fred Dallimore's family and our (McNutt) family are very good friends. Fred used to come up and run my baseball camp for me. Fred and his staff would also come up to umpire and help us out. Fred would come up and put on banquets for us. Fred Dallimore went out of his way to make sure that things went well for a lot of kids in the State of Nevada. He liked our kids and the make-up of our program, that's why he 'picked up' a lot of our kids. He has done a very good job at UNLV. It's a relationship that extends beyond the baseball diamond. It's just a great relationship."

Dustin Pedroia the 2008 American League MVP played for McNutt two summers.

Coach McNutt decided to coach again the 2009 season will mark his first in a non-Carson High uniform. He will be coaching the Galena Grizzlies in Reno. To show how much of a leader Coach McNutt is he has six former players on his coaching staff (Donovan Osborne, Tim Lichty, Ralph Clelan, Joe Hooft, Chris Utt, Jason Luttges) He even recruited a former head coach out of retirement from a rival school to help coach (Rob Hastings).

Coach John Savage graduated from Reno High School in 1983, was drafted by the New York Yankees in 1983, but opted to play at Santa Clara University from 1984 to 1986. He was then drafted by the Cincinnati Reds in 1986. He finished his playing career with the 1988 Reno Silver Sox squad. John Savage started his coaching career as the Reno High School pitching coach from 1988 to 1990, and then coached the Reno Knights in 1991 before becoming the pitching coach and recruiting coordinator at the University of Nevada from 1992 to 1996. He then was the pitching coach and recruiting coordinator at USC from 1996 to 2000 (USC won the College World Series in 1998). He worked as the head coach at UC Irvine from 2002 to 2004, and has worked as the head coach at UCLA since 2005.

He knew that baseball was going to be a major part of his life right away. He grew up in a baseball family and started playing baseball at age six, with older guys in his neighborhood. He played daily on the baseball fields at Swope Middle School in Reno and at Reno High School. Savage remembers, "I got engulfed in the baseball card scene and going to Reno Silver Sox games. Baseball was my passion."

Savage reminisced that Bud Beasley was, "a mentor to me; he took great interest in me as a pitcher. He would give me tips and he knew a lot of professional (baseball) people, many of which he would talk to about me. Bud was one of the best baseball people in my life. Bud Beasley was humble; he has a lot of energy. He has touched so many people. Bud Beasley is a big part of my baseball upbringing."

Coach Savage also remembers his Reno High School coach Bill Penaluna with admiration as he promoted the young Savage. Reno Silver Sox player Felix Oroz helped Savage hone his baseball skills. Tom House (San Diego Padres) "helped me every day after I signed my professional contract," Savage recalled.

Savage considered the decision to turn down the Yankee contract (1983) as a difficult one. "That (1983) was the breakout year for high school baseball players, Rob Richie, Matt Williams and I changed the way that professional scouts looked at Northern Nevada. The magic number, signing bonus wise, was $100,000, it was easy to turn down the money because I thought I would get stronger and healthier and I would be able to play for many more years; I was arrogant," Savage stated. Coach Savage said that part of his thinking was naive. "The telegram from George Steinbrenner hit me hard, it impressed me that the Yankees wanted me on their team," Savage said.

"My career was on the field and although it (my playing career) did not turn out the way I wanted, it did coaching wise."

After ending his playing career with the Reds, John Savage played one season for the Reno Silver Sox in 1988. Savage remembers, "It was a big change. I was on the downside of my career. I had arm problems. Being a member of an independent team in the Cal League was very tough. I was just trying to survive. I learned a lot about coaching from Nate Oliver." It seems to me that 1988 was a turning point in the baseball career of John Savage as it transformed him from being a pitcher to becoming a coach. He found success as a coach at the university level.

"The 1994 Nevada (Big West Champions) team opened the doors. We beat Fullerton. We won every series. The team had heart. Andy Dominique was a freshman. We went to the NCAA Central Regional in Austin, Texas. We were the number 2 seed in a regional where Oklahoma (the eventual National Champion) was the number 1 seed. We were almost dumb enough to think we could win it all," Coach Savage really enjoyed talking about the 1994 Nevada baseball team. Coach Savage has good memories about coaching with Nevada's head coach Gary Powers. "He never looked over my shoulders. He trusted me. We were together for 5 years. He taught me a lot about college baseball."

Coach Savage enjoys recruiting, "I love getting the best player available. I love hunting the guy down, showing him around the school and the facilities. I take (recruiting) personally. I love recruiting." Savage is very competitive and it shows through in his personality. He does not know the meaning of the word 'can't.' He is constantly on the prowl for the best player he can find. He works hard and watches a lot of video tape on players. He travels and constantly studies baseball players to ensure that he signs the very best player available.

As a coach, John Savage is equally competitive. "I like to teach (pitching) mechanics and the physical and mental sides of pitching", he explains. He has the tools and the ability to think quickly. He knows about baseball and what it takes to be a winner. He has a strong intellect and has the demeanor of the professional.

Savage has goals and a plan of where he's headed and how to get there. He is committed to his family and to the life of a major college coach. His strengths are obvious and it seems like his weaknesses are few. It was great to interview Coach Savage.

Index

Photo Credits

Photo Credits

CHAPTER	PAGE	SOURCE
8th Inning	85	UNLV Special Collections
	86	UNLV Special Collections
	87	Las Vegas 51s
	90	Las Vegas 51s
	96	Las Vegas 51s
	101	Arizona Diamondbacks
9th Inning	107 (top)	Tim Mueller
	107 (bottom)	Reno Aces
	108	Reno Aces
	110	Las Vegas 51s

Homeruns and Jackpots Order Form

Use this convenient order form to order additional copies
of
Homeruns and Jackpots

Please Print:

Name_____

Address_____

City_____ **State**_____

Zip_____

Phone(**)**_____

Email_____

_____ copies of book @ $11.95 each $_____
Postage and handling @ $2.50 per book $_____
NV residents add $1.03 tax per book $_____
Total amount enclosed $_____

Make checks and money orders payable to: Tim Mueller

Send order to: Tim Mueller
P.O. Box 2831 • Carson City, NV 89702-2831

Email: tim_mueller@sbcglobal.net